THE CATSKILLS
A Geological Guide

THE
CATSKILLS
A GEOLOGICAL GUIDE

Revised Edition by Robert Titus

Purple Mountain Press / Fleischmanns, New York

The Catskills: A Geological Guide
First published 1993
Revised edition 1998

Published by Purple Mountain Press, Ltd.
P.O. Box E3, Fleischmanns, New York 12430-0378
914-254-4062, 914-254-4476 (fax)
Purple@catskill.net
http://www.catskill.net/purple

Library of Congress Cataloging-in-Publication Data

Titus, Robert, 1946-
    The Catskills : a geological guide / by Robert Titus. - -Rev. ed.
      p.   cm.
    Includes index.
    ISBN 0-916346-65-X (pbk. : alk. paper)
      1. Geology- -New York (State)- -Catskill Mountains- -Guidebooks.
    2. Catskill Mountains (N.Y.)- -Guidebooks.   I. Title.
    QE146.C25T58   1998
    557.47'38- -dc21   98-42531
                                                          CIP

Frontispiece and title page: A Devonian forest by Charles
Knight, courtesy The Field Museum, Chicago, Illinois,
negative #73898.

Cover design by the author.

5 4 3 2 1

Manufactured in the United States of America.
Printed on acid-free paper.

Table of Contents

Chapter One

Exploring Time

The Present is a Key to the Past

NO ONE really understands the fourth dimension very well. All of us are stuck in one moment of time; it is called the present. We know that there are other times. In one direction time extends "in front" of us; we call that other time the future. In at least one other direction time extends "behind" us; we call that the past. You and I know about some of the past; we call it memory, but we cannot go there. We can anticipate being in the future, but when we get there (and that will usually take some time), it won't be the future anymore. It will have become the present, and the present is not the future. You see the trouble here.

It's a bit of a problem for scientists to be stuck in one time. If we could move around in that fourth dimension, science would advance far more rapidly. Of course, if we could move around in time, especially forward, then we wouldn't have to worry about how fast science is advancing. We would just zip forward and see how science had turned out. That would save a lot of work, but it wouldn't be much fun.

We humans like to put shorter brackets on time and provide names for the two ends of those brackets. We call the near past "history." The near past has people in it and they can write things down that we in the present can read. We call that "recorded history." The near future is inhabited too, and people there can write, but they can't send anything to us. That's why, in school, you didn't have to memorize what was going to happen, just the history that already had happened. Easier that way, but less practical.

Beyond the short brackets, we have longer stretches of time. The distant future is of no concern here, but the distant past is. Some people call it "deep time," but most of my colleagues and I like to call it "geological time." It is unrecorded history in the sense that nobody was there who could write it down. But, in a way, it is recorded: Recorded in the rocks. And that, generally, is what this book is about: The way in which we geologists read history from rocks.

Geologists have a unique vantage point in looking at time. More than any other group of scientists, we have developed an intuitive understanding of the fourth dimension of the universe. The world is about four and one half billion years old and a lot has happened here. Every spot that now exists on the surface of the globe has always existed, but in many, many different manifestations. Every place has a story to relate, and a very long story at that. Go outside and sit down anywhere and watch history pass by. See the birds and small animals, hear the wind and watch the grass grow. Dull stuff, maybe, but all of this is history; it's been going on for billions of years and sometimes it gets really exciting. Add a *Tyrannosaurus* or a saber-tooth tiger, and growing grass quickly becomes a great deal more interesting. Sadly, points on the surface of the globe are mute, and, exciting or dull, they cannot speak of their history. But every place does have a geology, and those rocks and sediments are a record of the past—a record which can be read, if you know how to do so.

The philosophy geologists have developed to guide them in their studies of the past is called "**uniformitarianism.**" It is most briefly explained in the phrase "the present is a key to the past." That is, we believe that the processes operating on the surface of the Earth today are essentially the same processes that have always been operating. Among these are weathering, erosion, climate, life and many others. Sometimes they operated faster and sometimes slower, but they have remained, through time, always the same ongoing processes. That's what is uniform about uniformitarianism.

The practical essence of all of this is that we believe that today's sedimentary rocks were the sediments of the past and that they formed in ancient sedimentary environments that we can learn about and understand. Thus, we geologists study the present, especially present-day sediments, and then we apply what we have learned to the rock record in order to deduce the history found there. And so the present is a key to the past. We can do this in the Catskills. Let me demonstrate:

An Elevator Through Time

Slide Mountain is the highest summit in the Catskills (4,180 ft.) and has one of the finest views in the region. Perhaps you've been to the top of Slide Mountain and know its summit. Imagine for a moment that there is a door to an elevator shaft up there. This is a time elevator, built for geologists to take them back into the Catskills' distant past. This elevator takes you down into the Earth, through the many layers of rock that make up Slide. You don't stop at floors; you stop at moments in time. There are four doors, each facing one of the four compass directions. When the elevator stops at a particular ancient moment, one or more doors open upon the landscape as it was then. The only flaw is that this elevator can take you only to those moments of time that are recorded within the strata of the Catskills.

We go in, push a button, and down we go. The first leg of our trip is not very long and not very far. The east-facing door opens only a few feet beneath the surface. But those few feet have taken us far into the past, to a time geologists call the **Devonian Period**. It's 350 million years ago and out there is a mountain range, called the Acadian Mountains, rising above where the Berkshires are today. It's hard to tell from where we are, but the snow-capped peaks appear to tower tens of thousands of feet above sea level. These are young mountains, recently uplifted. Below the white peaks, the colors grade downward from dark blue to purple to red to rose. The near slopes are dry, barren of plants, and shimmering in the heat of a high sun. In the foreground lies an enormous deposit of sand and gravel. The surface is scarred with rills and gullies, but there's no water; it's been dry for a very long time and stream flow is rare.

The elevator's east door closes and the west one opens. The landscape it reveals slopes gently westward. There are a few more dry stream channels, and a primitive yellow green foliage struggles along the dry banks.

The west door closes and down we go. A short trip takes us another thousand feet, down to 362 million years ago. The east door opens and we view an active river flowing toward us. It's at high water but not flooding, and the currents flow smoothly and silently. On the horizon above are the remnants of once-great mountains. They are the same mountains we saw at the last stop, but now they are in a much different state. This has been a time of no crustal uplift and the pause has allowed them to crumble into the rounded skyline profile that we see. Storm clouds mask the upper reaches; it is raining up there.

Suddenly, the south door opens and we see a dense jungle of primitive plants. They are unlike anything we see today. The upper limbs have a "fur" of short, simple leaves that look like green scales. Below the limbs, the tree trunks are ornamented with the scars left when similar leaves fell to the ground. The weedy ground crawls with centipedes, spiders and other "bugs." At least these are familiar. There is something wrong here, but it takes a few moments to notice: The jungle here should be screaming with noise, but it is as quiet as can be—unnervingly so. The air is perfectly still and there is no rustling of the leaves. There are no animals or birds, and without them, there is a silence here that is unknown in any modern forest.

The doors shut and down we go, another 500 feet. This time all four doors open at once and we see a shallow sea floor, but no water floods in; our elevator won't allow that. It's 378 million years ago, and around us heavily armored, sluggish fish-like creatures swim close to the bottom. Only the presence of primitive clumsy-looking fins confirms that these are indeed fish. This marine world begins to look a little more familiar when we see that the sea floor is littered with clams and snails, but the rest of the shellfish defy description in what is a most remarkably alien sea bottom.

Figure 1-1: Primitive fish.
Courtesy New York State Museum.

The doors close and we resume our descent. When they open, it is 381 million years ago. Once again we are surrounded by ocean, but this time the water is deep and it is nearly black all around. We are soon overwhelmed by a fetid, sulfurous stench and our elevator starts to warm up uncomfortably. The sea around us is stagnant, tepid, and dead. As our eyes become adjusted to the dim light we are gradually able to discern an image. A partly decomposed corpse of an enormous jellyfish appears and hangs, nearly motionless, in our field of view. The sight is repulsive and we quickly close the doors. Down we go.

After another trip we reach 393 million years ago at a depth of nearly 8,000 feet beneath the top of Slide Mountain. We are more than a mile down, well below sea level. Again all four of our elevator doors open and we gaze out onto what initially looks like a meadow, but is really a very shallow sea floor. The brightly sunlit sandy bottom is white and dotted with the green of marine algae. Beautiful creatures rise above the algae. They are simple animals with the odd name of "sea lilies." The name is appropriate, however, for they have long stems and are rooted into the sand bottom. At the top of each of the long stems are five brightly colored, delicately branched arms. As gentle marine currents pass across this meadow, the arms of the sea lilies seem to grasp at the waters, as if reaching for food.

The doors all shut once again. Shortly, when they re-open, we look out upon a bleak coastal landscape. All around us are broad tidal flats. Although they were flooded recently, now they are baking in the sun. All around, mats of dark, green-brown, leathery algae are rotting and stinking in the sun. In between the algal mats are pools of salt water brine.

Figure 1-2: Sea lily.
Courtesy New York
State Museum.

Figure 1-3: Jellyfish.

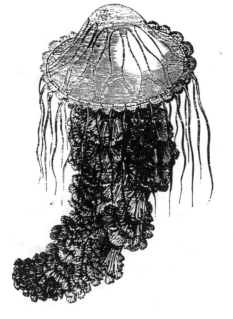

They have been drying out and are rimmed by deposits of salt. This is a quiet, desolate and dead place, but it is an important landscape. This is the goal of our journey. These are the oldest sediments of the Catskill sequence and this landscape, bleak as it is, marks the very beginning of Catskill history, 394 million years ago.

Our elevator ride of the mind's eye is over; our elevator will go no lower. This was an exciting adventure to contemplate, and you will be tempted to dismiss it as an impossibility, something best left to science fiction, since time elevators do not exist and never will. But that is not entirely true. There is, in fact, no such elevator at the top of Slide Mountain, but the Catskills themselves constitute one grand elevator ride through time. And it's quite a bit better than the one we traveled in. It's not a small box, but instead some of the prettiest landscape in all the world.

This book is intended to be a ride in that real time elevator. We will travel far more slowly and, this time, we will travel by car and by foot.

Figure 1-4: Devonian seascape.

How to Use This Book

Chances are good that you enjoy the outdoors; otherwise you would not be likely to read this book. All of us can appreciate the beauty of nature, and there is an awful lot of that in the Catskills. However, your natural appreciation of the outdoors is something that can be greatly improved and refined. A geological field guide can show you how much more you can see and appreciate as you hike the trails of the Catskills, especially the history that is recorded in our rocks and landscapes.

The normal plan of a field guide is to present the reader with a series of pictures with names and brief descriptions. That procedure works quite well with birds, trees, and shells, but with geology you need a lot more. You can see from the introductory field trip that there is quite a story behind the history of our rocks, and that more than simple pictures and descriptions are needed. I'd rather you not worry about accumulating a pile of specimens. Instead it would be better for you to be able to accumulate an understanding of our Catskill bedrock geology. This book is a brief and basic introduction. Its focus is to develop a broad but introductory understanding of our Catskill geology and to give you a "feel" for our Catskill landscape. I simply intend that you develop a meaningful sense of what you can see in our Catskill rocks.

So how do you do it? If you want to, you can read my book from cover to cover. That is certainly a good way to start, but that is not necessarily the best way to understand our Catskill geology. I will let you in on a secret of science: We scientists rarely read books from cover to cover, but choose to "browse" our books instead. We read the sections which are of most interest to us, perhaps several times, and then reach for the next book. You see, science is so vast that there is no way that you can, or even need to, know it all. Instead, you focus on that which is of the greatest interest to you at the time. It's much less of a chore that way. So read the book through and then go back and browse the sections that appeal to you the most.

The book is set up for browsing. Chapter 5 is theoretical material describing the mountain-building processes that have affected the Catskill region. Although it's helpful background knowledge, it is not field-oriented. Real field guide topics are found in the other chapters. Chapters 3, 4, 6 and 8 describe the different masses of rock that make up the Catskills. These focus on how you can read from them the records of their ancient environments. They explain how geologists develop images of the past from rocks. Chapters 7 and 9 describe the fossils of the region, the land and sea creatures that inhabited those prehistoric environments. Each chapter is subdivided into numerous sections. You can quickly find those topics that appeal to you and skip those that don't.

That's it: Mountain-building, rocks, fossils, and ancient environments. You will, I think, have a pretty good understanding of the bedrock geology of the Catskills once you have mastered a basic understanding of these categories.

The glacial history of the region is a fascinating story, but is not treated in this book. I have written another book on that subject, also published by Purple Mountain Press.

I have made this guide as thoroughly illustrated as my talents allow. Pictures are vital and you will want to spend some time studying them. In fact, to do things well, you should spend a lot of time with this guide before you go outside. Keep the guide handy and browse through it whenever you are in the mood. Read the sections that interest you several times, and you will be surprised at how quickly you become comfortable with this material. And that's the time to go outside.

Don't be too shy about plunging into this science. Geology is not rocket science; instead, it is a field that almost everyone is able to enjoy. And I mean that; I want you to have fun with my science. The Catskill Park has a fine system of hiking trails. My science will help you see a lot more when you are out there.

Equipment

You won't need to be too well equipped. Deck yourself out in hiking clothes and, if you need to, equip yourself with good camping gear. Beyond that, there are just a few things you might bring along: Certainly a camera, and a compass is a necessity if you plan to hike off the marked trails. You will be tempted to bring a hammer and a chisel, but they will probably not be necessary. I rarely bring them and it's quite unusual for me to see anything that I really need to bring home. The Catskills are a great outdoor museum. Only the rarest specimens should be brought indoors, and then only for their protection.

Maps are probably the single most valuable pieces of equipment if you plan to do a lot of outdoor geology. The 7.5-minute quadrangle maps, published by the United States Geological Survey, are of great value and are available for all areas of the Catskills. I also recommend the maps published by the New York-New Jersey Trail Conference for the Catskill Park area. They are good, rugged maps, meant for the outdoors, tear- and water-resistant, and they don't soil easily. The Catskill Center for Conservation and Development at Arkville publishes an excellent map of the entire Catskill region. Look for all of these at camping or hunting and fishing stores.

Hazards

There are dangers in any outdoor recreation. Common sense is always the best guard against injury; if something scares you, don't do it! Be careful of wet slopes, avoid icy conditions, and have a real respect for steep hills and cliffs. With good judgment you should have little trouble. But bad luck strikes everybody eventually, so I urge you always to hike with friends or at least let somebody know where you are going and when you should be back.

Other Resources

You should visit the New York State Museum in Albany. The museum houses a very fine collection of geological materials, much of which is on display. The Geological Survey of the State Museum has a number of publications on state geology, many that are suitable for the amateur. Many of the best New York State Museum publications are out of print so you might check your local library or used book stores to see if they have them.

Chapter Two

Reading Rocks

ONE of our favorite stories in geology, passed down through the generations, is about James Hutton's visit to Siccar Point. Hutton was a brilliant professor of geology at the University of Edinburgh during the 1790s. That was a remarkable time in the intellectual circles of Scotland, a time commonly remembered as the "Scottish Renaissance." Hutton is regarded as a leading figure of that renaissance. For some time he had been contemplating the age of the Earth. He reckoned that rivers carved their own valleys, and that it must have taken them an extremely long time to do so. From that he deduced that the world beneath rivers must itself be unfathomably old. But how old is that?

Hutton never would find out the age of the Earth, but he would be struck, perhaps the word is "thunderstruck," by the enormity of the length of that time. This moment occurred on his trip to Siccar Point on an island off Scotland. Although Hutton did not know it as he sailed toward it, the Siccar Point vicinity has had a complex history over the past half-billion years. Here, from time to time, oceans have inundated the landscape and deposited their sediments. Also, from time to time, the Siccar Point area has lain adjacent to rising mountains and has had enormous quantities of sediment shed upon it from their erosion. In short, on his way to Siccar Point Hutton did not yet understand the venerable history of our planet. Back then, nobody did.

When he reached Siccar Point, Hutton saw three geological units: The modern sandy sediment on the floor of the present-day sea, and two units of rocks which once had themselves been sediments. Hutton instantly recognized that the three units presented him with the records of three fragments of time. They represented three sedimentary environments and also three moments in Earth history: The present-day moment of time with its modern ocean and recent sediments, and two ancient moments of time with their sedimentary environments and their sediments. The latter two were separated by an erosional surface which indicated a long period when that surface was a landscape subject to the vicissitudes of weathering and erosion. Still another long period of time lay between the second of these two ancient environments and the modern world.

What Hutton had looked at were rocks; what he had seen was history. His mind, at that moment and at that place, flew back dizzyingly through vast lengths of time to those ancient worlds. That was when and where mankind came to understand geological time.

Hutton and geology would never be the same again. Hutton would go on to become the founding father of uniformitarianism with its intense sense of time, and the science of geology would become devoted to exploring the depths of that time, Earth history.

We can learn much about the nature of both science and genius from this story. It's easy to explain Hutton's science; almost anybody can grasp his discovery. That's typical of most science; it's not really all that hard to understand. Genius is the hard part. What takes genius in science is to be the first person to make a great discovery or to think a great thought. What's good about this is that the rest of us don't have to be geniuses. We can almost always come to understand the great discoveries of science, be enlightened by them, and enjoy that enlightenment.

Today the geological time traveler can recreate Hutton's great moment at Siccar Point. You can do that anytime and anywhere if only you understand the local rocks. We began doing just that in the last chapter with our elevator ride at Slide Mountain. Like Hutton, we can peer backwards through time when we look at our Catskill strata. Today these rocks make up the modern Catskill Mountain range. But surprisingly, as we saw in the last chapter, they record the history of a much older mountain landscape, that western New England range you had probably never heard of: The **Acadian Mountains**. Those mountains reached elevations that may have rivaled those of the Himalayas. Catskill sedimentary rocks also record the history of an ancient sea that lay just west of the Acadians, a sea that occupied a great depression in the Earth's surface called the **Appalachian Basin**. It's sometimes called the **Catskill Sea**, but I will use several terms to describe it, based on the three masses of sedimentary rocks that accumulated within it: First, the **Helderberg Sea**, with its thick sequences of gray limestone;, then the **poison sea**, a mass of black shale; and finally, the **Hamilton Sea**, which is mostly brown sandstone.

Those ancient seas produced a great deal of sedimentary rocks, but, most of all, Catskill strata record the presence of a huge delta complex that once existed. Devonian rivers descended the slopes of the Acadians and deposited the sediments of the fabled **Catskill Delta**. This enormous heap of sandstone and shale is one of the best-preserved ancient deltas in the fossil record. It is world famous, and it should be. This delta is the center of our story; it has a wonderful story to read.

Chapter Three

The Helderberg Sea

A Tropical Paradise

IF you have ever been to Florida, you have seen its stunning white and soft pink beaches and aqua-colored waters. Pink and aqua are the colors of the seas that produce **limestones**. Among the world's most common sedimentary rocks, these are composed largely of the ground-up shells of ancient fossil organisms. Shells are mostly composed of calcium carbonate ($CaCO_3$), and that is the mineralogy of limestones. It is because of their mineralogy that they are easily identified. Calcium carbonate is too soft to scratch glass and it effervesces in hydrochloric acid, which is marketed as muriatic acid. A field geologist will often carry some of this acid in a small medicine bottle with an eye dropper in order to do the "acid test" for this type of rock.

Limestones are a thing of the past! Well, almost. Throughout geological time, limestones have been one of the most common types of sedimentary rocks. They are not today. But, as good geologists, we are going to apply the principle of uniformitarianism in order to understand these rocks of the past. So let's begin this section on limestones by learning about where they form today. And the answer is: "In very nice places."

You see, limestones are typical of shallow tropical seas, and where those seas have sandy shorelines, people see them as being very nice places indeed. The two locations that immediately come to mind are Florida and the Bahamas. There are other shallow tropical seas, such as the Coral Sea and Persian Gulf, but not many

Americans have been to these places, so they are not likely to be well known to readers of this tome.

But if you have been to either Florida or the Bahamas, you can quickly recollect some very nice images of soft pink sands adjacent to some particularly clear and aqua-colored waters. If you have ventured out on a boat, you may remember that the water depths are quite shallow even a long distance offshore. This is especially true of the Bahamas and the western and southern coasts of Florida, where it is commonplace to be able to see to the bottom even miles offshore. If you have gone snorkeling or, better still, scuba diving in such seas, then you can, no doubt, vividly recall some splendidly rich sea floor ecologies—real Jacques Cousteau seascapes. If you have not had the privilege of such experiences—and most people haven't been so fortunate—then I hope you have seen film or photos of such seascapes, because you need to have at least some such background to conjure up the right images for the limestones of the Catskill region. Hard as it is to imagine, it is still true that a trip on Rt. 20 eastward from Cherry Valley or a hike along the crest of the ridge at the John Boyd Thacher State Park takes you through some of the finest tropical seascapes that have ever existed!

The Limestone Formations

In the Catskills the two major groups of Devonian limestones are the **Helderberg** and **Onondaga** Limestones, both named after locations where they are especially well exposed. Each of these groups is divided into smaller units called **formations**. I am going to describe the first three formations of the Helderberg Group because they illustrate some of the basics for understanding (or "reading") the rocks, as done by geologists.

The first is the **Manlius Limestone** (figure 3-1), named after the town of Manlius, which is located east of Syracuse. This is a "Persian Gulf" limestone. By that I mean that these sediments were originally deposited along a dry, tropical coast much like that along the shores of the Persian Gulf today. The unit is a very fine-grained one, which means that the sediments were originally

Facing page:.

Figure 3-1: The Manlius Limestone.

Typical, thick-bedded ledges.

Figure 3-2 (right): The Manlius Limestone.

Lower strata are typical thick-bedded ledges, upper strata are laminated algal beds.

Figure 3-3 (below): Closeup of the Coeymans Limestone showing thick bedding and abundant crinoid ossicles.

(See figures 1-3 and 7-11.)

composed of grains in the silt and clay size range. That's small, and when the sediment hardens it becomes a rock with individual grains that are much too tiny to be seen: A fine-grained rock.

Two environments of deposition were responsible for accumulating the sediments of the Manlius. The first was the shallow subtidal setting that lay along the shore, and the second was the adjacent onshore, supratidal mud flats. These flats lay just barely above sea level and were commonly subject to flooding during especially high tides and unusual storms. All of this is typical of what we see today along the shores of the Persian Gulf, especially its Saudi Arabian side.

I said earlier that limestones form in nice places, but the Manlius Limestone immediately makes me a liar. Neither of its sedimentary settings was a particularly nice place during the early Devonian. In fact, each must have been a downright unpleasant location. The near-shore setting was shallow and subject to the baking of the tropical sun. It must have been very hot.

This shallow coastal sea was tidal and the tides swept back and forth daily across a broad tidal flat. With a hot and arid climate, the tidal flat was inhospitable, to say the least. Think about it: At high tide you are submerged under hot salt water; at low tide you are exposed to the broiling tropical sun. Few organisms could tolerate this setting, and consequently very few fossil species are found in the Manlius Limestone. Algae, however, were sometimes common. These most primitive of "plants" had been around for several billion years by the dawn of the Devonian, and they had evolved a tolerance for all sorts of unlikely conditions, including salty, broiling mud flats. The algae grew into sheets that are not well preserved. But when present they do give the rock a thinly laminated, ribbony appearance (figure 3-2). These traits are common and should be looked for.

The **Coeymans Limestone** (pronounced coo-ee-mans) is different (figure 3-3), having been deposited in a shallow, open sea floor that lay offshore of the Manlius coast. The Coeymans was indeed deposited in a nice place, a hospitable sea floor where plants and animals flourished. That's what makes the Coeymans a different and, I think, far more interesting unit of rock. The Coeymans is a coarse-grained limestone formed of sandy sediments that are mixed with a large number of whole and broken shells. It's thicker-bedded as well, suggesting a more wave-swept and current-swept environment of deposition. The real story of the Coeymans is in its fossil faunas, but I'll discuss them in Chapter Seven.

The third formation is the **Kalkberg Limestone** (figure 3-4). The Kalkberg formed even farther offshore, in deeper and quieter waters. It's those latter conditions that had the greatest influence on the Kalkberg. Once again this is a fine-grained sedimentary rock that was originally a mud. Muds are mixtures of silt and clay-sized particles. This unit is thin-bedded and is the product of brief episodes of deposition by weak, gentle currents.

Of particular interest within the Kalkberg are the chert nodules (figures 3-6 and 3-7). Look for these shiny, blue or brown-black, irregular nodules occurring in horizons within the strata of the Kalkberg. Chert is better known as flint and is formed by chemical processes within the original sediments.

Each of these units records a brief episode of Earth history which geologists piece together to reconstruct whole chapters of history. We can do that with the Helderberg Group limestones. These first three units of the Helderberg, the Manlius, Coeymans and Kalkberg, fall into a historical sequence: The first was coastal, the second formed near shore, and the third was offshore. That defines a marine transgression, a deepening of the sea as it invades and submerges a vicinity. **Transgressions** are commonly found in the rock record, as are their opposites, the **regressions**. I'll be describing a fine regression later on.

Most of the rocks above the Helderberg Group are shales and sandstones, but there is one more important unit of limestone, called the Onondaga Limestone (figure 3-5). You won't have much trouble identifying the Onondaga, with its light gray limestone and thick-bedding entirely unlike the Helderberg. It often has quite a few chert nodules within it (figures 3-6 & 7), and this chert was very commonly used by Indian craftsmen to produce stone implements. But the standout features of the Onondaga are its fossil coral reefs. More on them in Chapter Seven.

Figure 3-4 (above): Typical Kalkberg Limestone.
The bedding is generally thin and uniform.

Facing page from the top.

Figure 3-5: Onondaga Limestone showing typical thick ledges.

Figure 3-6: Chert nodules.

Figure 3-7: Chert nodules.

Figure 3-8: John Boyd Thacher State Park.
Minelot Falls and the trail below. Base of Devonian just above trail.
Courtesy New York State Museum.

Field Trips to the Helderberg Sea

The Indian Ladder: Like old houses that have survived the tests of time, the Catskill Mountains are built upon a foundation of sturdy stone. This is the above-described Helderberg Limestone, an unusually dense and solid bedrock. The Helderberg can be seen as a band of bedrock that forms a resistant ridge, just west of the Hudson River. You can see it along Rt. 9W for quite some distance south of Saugerties. It also extends north to the town of Catskill, and from there, to Ravena. Here and there it is quarried for cement. Beyond Ravena, the unit trends off to the northwest, creating its most impressive ledge, the Helderberg Mountains, which overlook Albany. The most scenic stretch of the Helderberg Mountains is the "Indian Ladder," an 80-foot-tall limestone cliff perched atop an escarpment at John Boyd Thacher State Park (figure 3-8). The name commemorates the trunk of a pine tree, which supposedly served as a ladder here long ago. From the park, the Helderberg Limestone extends to the west to Syracuse, and beyond to Seneca Falls.

Thacher Park was a gift to the state by Emma Treadwell Thacher in 1914, in honor of her late husband, who was once mayor of Albany. The park was intended primarily to be a place of recreation as well as a campground and animal preserve. Originally, the park was only 350 acres, but it has grown considerably since 1914.

The top of the escarpment has a grand scenic view. Enter the park from the east on Rt. 157 and pull into "Cliff Edge Overlook." From that site, on a clear day you can see the Berkshire Mountains to the east, the Adirondacks to the north, and the Albany vicinity, which lies only about 10 miles to the northeast.

Geology is our chief draw at Thacher, however. Leave the overlook parking lot and drive west a short distance to the Lagrange Bush picnic area. From that site you can get a good, close-up look at the escarpment.

The cliffs are made up of the two basal units of the Helderberg, the Manlius and Coeymans Limestones. Both are hard and dense, and they are very effective cliff-makers. You can conveniently visit both of them by taking the Indian Ladder Trail, which wanders about a quarter-mile along the base of the cliff (figure 3-8). I like to descend the eastern staircase and head west. This simple staircase is a time machine; as you descend the steps, you are traveling back to the dawn of the Devonian period, a little more than 400 million years ago.

Go down two flights of stairs, and you will encounter a horizontal notch that has been cut into some relatively soft horizons of the Manlius Limestone. The notch is called the "Upper Bear Path," and it can be traced across the whole park. There are about 40 feet of the Manlius Limestone below the notch, and nine more above it. That makes the Upper Bear Path an excellent marker bed, and geologists use it to orient themselves as they explore the length of the escarpment.

The Manlius is mostly a blue-gray, very fine-grained limestone. At first glance there is very little that catches the eye, and it might seem that these rocks have no good story to tell. But they do. If you want to continue on the trail you must bend down to pass through the notch. On your way through, turn over and look up at the underside of the overhang. You will see a faint and delicate polygonal pattern (similar to figure 8-10). It's not obvious, so do look carefully. These polygons are **mud cracks**. Once this rock was the soft, wet sediment of a mud flat, baking in a hot sun. As it dried up, it shrank and split into these mud-crack polygons. By themselves, mud cracks tell us only a little about what it was like here at the dawn of the Devonian Period. They make up a single bit of evidence, but that evidence is a start. You have begun to read the story within the rocks.

Now comes the hard part: There is a massive nine-foot-thick limestone above the ledge, and another massive eight-foot ledge below. If you look carefully, you can see that these strata are fossiliferous. A delicate pattern defines a number of fossils called **stromatoporoids**. Since they don't photograph well, I am showing you a photo published first by the New York State Museum (figure 3-9). Stromatoporoids are long extinct, and we really don't know what they were, but most paleontologists relate them to primitive corals or sponges. They certainly were reef-building invertebrates, and knowing that gives us more clues with which to work.

Throughout the Manlius sequence you will see thinly-laminated limestone beds, sometimes called **ribbon limestone** or **rhythmites**. The beds of the Upper Bear Path, and most of the strata just below the lower stromatoporoid beds, are laminated. Not surprisingly, it was a long time before anybody paid much heed to these nondescript structures, but back in the 1960s it was first suggested that these were actually fossils of an odd sort. They were recognized as being fossil blue-green algae that grew in thin sheets called **algal mats** (figure 3-2), which hardened into rock. Since then we have learned that these primitive microbes are actually more properly called blue-green bacteria than "algae," but the older name has stuck.

Figure 3-9: Stromatoporoids.
Courtesy New York State Museum.

The algal mats give us some very important evidence about the ancient environment, and now we can begin to see the story at Thacher Park emerging. The Manlius Limestone was deposited in a complex environment. First, there were the broad mud flats. During all or at least part of the day these flats were exposed to an intense sun, and the mud cracks formed. This would have been a very unpleasant place for most living creatures, but the blue-green "algae" flourished in this harsh habitat and grew in dense mats.

The mud flats were not good places for reef-building animals to live, however. The two stromatoporoid beds mark the two times when, for reasons we cannot explain, the waters abruptly deepened. The mud flats suddenly gave way to shallow, subtidal environments. Here, twice a day, during high tides, marine waters rose up and brought sustenance to the interesting marine invertebrate ecosystems of the stromatoporoid reefs that flourished here. They grew into what became quite substantial reefs.

If you use a little imagination, you can conjure up quite an image of what it must have been like here during the Devonian. The setting was certainly tropical; thick limestones form only in tropical or subtropical settings. Let me add a little color to the picture for you. The algae would have been a dark brownish-green. They would not have smelled very good, especially after baking in the sun for a while. The sediments are likely to have been quite bright, maybe even white, perhaps with a pinkish tint. Sadly, these sediments have turned gray with age. The transparent aqua waters would have been the most beautiful aspect of the landscape. We will never know what color the stromatoporoids might have been.

Continue westward on the Indian Ladder Trail. Following the trail, you will continue to descend for a while longer. Remember that you are still traveling backwards through time. On your way down, you should watch for more algal mats.

Soon you will reach Minelot Falls (figure 3-8). At its base is another well-defined notch. The soft strata that make up the notch define the Rondout Limestone. There are no fossils in the Rondout, but the unit is very important. It does not belong to the Devonian Period, but to the earlier Silurian. The boundary of these two important time units is right here; you can almost put your finger on it. The first of the resistant layers making up the ledge above the Rondout approximates the dawn of the Devonian. We geologists tend to get excited when we see horizons of rock of such historic significance.

To the lover of the Catskills, however, this horizon has an even greater significance. This ledge defines not only the dawn of the Devonian, but also the dawn of the whole Catskill sequence itself. You are looking at what was literally the beginning of Catskill history. This horizon, once sediment, marks the very first deposit of what would be the whole Catskill sequence. This single stratum extends underneath the surface all across the Catskills. It's usually buried under hundreds or even thousands of feet of sedimentary rocks. For about 50 million years, layer upon layer of sediment was deposited upon it in an increasingly thick heap. Thus, the thousands of feet of shales and sandstones that make up our mountains slowly piled up upon this horizon. Thacher Park is one of the few places where we can truly see the very beginnings of the Catskills, and that is a most remarkable thing to ponder while visiting the park.

But, back to the trail: Continue west, and the trail begins an ascent. As you climb the stairway, you will pass the Upper Bear Path once again. About nine feet above it, the limestone changes to a more massively bedded and coarser-grained rock. Our staircase time machine has brought us to the Coeymans Limestone.

This limestone has a very different story to tell from that of the Manlius. The Coeymans is usually richly fossiliferous with the shellfish (Chapter Seven) that once inhabited what geologists call a shallow shelf environment. This shelf was a clear, aqua-colored, very shallow tropical sea. Its marine ecosystem was very rich. Sadly, I was disappointed in how few fossils I could find in the Coeymans here—almost none. However, as I left the trail, I did observe some fine fossil corals. Look for the "#1—On the Trail" sign. Just about three feet below it are some very good corals. I found some more Coeymans fossils west of the Indian Ladder Trail, on the trail above the escarpment.

Just before the western end of the Indian Ladder Trail is a small pavilion with a bronze plaque honoring the many early geologists who visited the site and studied these limestones. I thought this was a nice touch.

The Old Highway

My favorite place to see the limestones of the western Catskills is along U.S. Rt. 20. This venerable federal highway was once one of our nation's premier superhighways. It was one of the first coast-to-coast auto routes, and in its day it was just as important as the legendary Rt. 66. It's just not as well remembered today as that other road, probably because nobody wrote a song about it. Anyway, to see the limestones, join Rt. 20 northeast of Cherry Valley where it intersects with Otsego County Rt. 166. Within a mile of this intersection are all sorts of excellent exposures of the Helderberg and Onondaga Limestones. This vicinity is one of the great geologic tourist traps of the East. Anybody who is anybody in geology has been here.

Use the Rt. 20 and Rt. 166 intersection as a starting point. Travel half a mile north on 166 and you will come to a tall cliff of limestone on the eastern side of the road. The lower 50 feet or so make up the Manlius Limestone. All of this is fine-grained limestone. Watch for the ribbony algal limestone at the base of the outcrop. Several horizons display the empty casts of ancient mud flat crystals. Fossil hunting is poor, but several forms can be obtained (Chapter Seven). There are no stromatoporoids here.

As you work your way up the road from the base of the outcrop, you will observe that the strata become coarser-grained and sandy-looking and the beds are thicker as well. Here fossil hunting is quite a bit better. This is the Coeymans Limestone and it is a lot of fun to explore this unit. Once this was a shallow water, wave- and current-swept marine ecology. Its rich fossil fauna had heavy shells that were robust enough for this rugged sea floor.

Head a short distance south again. Just before the Rt. 20 bridge, you will see another fine exposure of the Coeymans Limestone where the rock is positively rich in fossils.

Continue south; just beyond the bridge is an outcrop of the Kalkberg Limestone. Look for a thinner-bedded and finer-grained limestone. Fossil hunting can be good here; watch for shellfish with very delicate skeletons. This was a deeper-water sea floor with quiet water conditions. Robust shells were not needed.

Head east on Rt. 20. Just before and slightly beyond the abandoned railroad bridge are more fine exposures of the Kalkberg Limestone. The best fossil hunting is on the north side of the road. Watch for quite a few chert nodules in the rocks here.

From six-tenths of a mile to one full mile east of Rt. 166 on Rt. 20, you will find cliffs of the Onondaga Limestone. This thickly-bedded, fine-grained limestone is fossiliferous throughout, but it is so hard and brittle that fossil collecting is nearly impossible. Do watch for the extensive fossil corals in the lower levels of this unit. There are so many of these that you might call this a fossil coral reef. About half a mile south of the junction of Rt. 166 and Rt. 20 there are more coral-rich exposures of the Onondaga.

Continuing east on Rt. 20 you will find, from place to place, more exposures of the Coeymans, Kalkberg and Onondaga limestones. The fossil hunting is sometimes very good. You will also see some very dark black shales. They represent a much different environment from that of the tropical paradise.

Chapter Four

The Poison Sea

CONTRARY to the stereotype, most scientists have rich imaginations, and we often like to indulge in wild speculations about our fields of research. Most of the time these ideas can be quickly proven wrong, but sometimes we get an off-the-wall idea that is not so easily eliminated, and in fact it may start to look pretty good. Such an idea, called a hypothesis, needs a lot of work, but if it survives a long period of careful investigation and still looks good we call it a theory. Speculation, hypothesis, theory: All this provides us with a step-by-step framework in which to do science. But we must be patient because these steps take time and work.

Recently, an interesting new hypothesis was introduced that may offer us a chance to better understand the rocks that lie above the limestones of the lower Catskill sequence. These are black shales and dark sandstones. The dark appearance of these strata makes them remarkably eye-catching and they loom, dark and menacing, over the landscapes wherever they are exposed. They can be seen along Rt. 20, but they are best exposed in the Hudson Valley.

Black stratified rocks are often rich in undecayed organic matter; it's the black of the carbon that gives these rocks their color. This generally suggests to the geologist that there were low-oxygen conditions in the sea waters at the time of deposition. Without oxygen, most decay bacteria cannot function and they soon die. But why low oxygen? That's where the new hypothesis comes in.

This new idea is sometimes called the "killer-tree hypothesis." Although the term may seem a little too extravagant, it probably isn't that far off the mark. The story starts during the middle Devonian, when the evolution of land plants was really starting to accelerate. By then land plants had been around for quite some time, but they had managed to evolve only into small forms with thin, weak stems. Nothing that could be called a tree had yet appeared. Trees require wood as support tissue. Not surprisingly, when wood did evolve, large, tall land plants soon followed and the world's first forests quickly appeared (see Chapter Nine).

So what do trees on land have to do with black-colored shales in the ocean? Quite a bit, it turns out. Wood has much to do with our story because it allowed trees to grow so tall that they required deep root systems, and that's when we return to the black shale and the poison sea. Complex root systems help to break up bedrock and they greatly accelerate the rate at which bedrock is weathered into soils. Not surprisingly, then, deep, well-developed soils appeared in the Devonian, possibly for the first time. This was a major transformation of the landscape. Barren landscapes with thin soils were soon replaced by lush foliage and thick soils as our world's landscapes turned green and blossomed with plants that grew in deep soils.

All of this led to far more rapid rates of deposition in nearby oceans. Thick soils were easily eroded and provided sediments that glutted nearby streams. The sediments were eventually transported into the nearest ocean, which was the Catskill Sea. All of this material was rich in dissolved nutrients, materials such as nitrates and phosphates. When these nutrient-rich sediments entered the Catskill Sea, they fertilized the water, and that led to the next step in what was now a complex chain of events.

The newly fertilized oceans were ideal for algae; they experienced what is called "**algal blooms**." Great population explosions of algae occurred in the shallow, surface waters of the Catskill Sea. While all this was great for the algae, it was tragic for just about every other category of marine organisms. As the algae died, they were attacked by decay bacteria. The decay process consumed so much oxygen that the seas soon became oxygen-depleted. With the loss of oxygen, bacteria had in effect poisoned their own habitat. Because they needed oxygen too, their numbers soon plummeted, and very soon all types of animals suffocated in the oxygen-depleted sea as well. But the algae just kept on proliferating in the surface waters where there was plenty of oxygen, diffusing in from the air. Soon, large masses of undecayed algal material sank to the floor of the ocean. Almost none of this biological matter ever decayed; consequently, the sediments that are found there are very rich in black organic carbon. These would eventually harden into thinly laminated, black shales of the "**poison sea**."

When this happens today in a closed body of water we refer to it as **eutrophication**. The Catskill Sea was largely isolated from other deep bodies of water. In its early history it was nearly surrounded by land or very shallow water (figure 5-1A). To its east, land blocked weather patterns and shielded the basin from much storm activity. The climate was tropical and the coastal lowlands provided lots of vegetation, much of which drifted into the basin. This vegetation contributed more organic matter that helped the algae in the creation of the black shales.

All of these conditions promoted what are called thermally-stratified and stagnant waters. The surface layer was hot while, at depths, the lower strata of water remained cool. Dense mats of floating plants and animals grew upon the warm surface waters. We refer to a drifting and floating ecology as "planktonic," similar to that of today's Sargasso Sea. Depth stratification and a dense planktonic mat prevented agitation and mixing of the waters, causing stagnant sea floor conditions to develop. The only fossils preserved in such a setting are those of planktonic organisms whose skeletons settled to the bottom after death.

Soon a deep basin with a black mud bottom, devoid of life, appeared. Virtually nothing could live in this sea, except at the surface where there was always plenty of oxygen. This was truly the poison sea.

Stratigraphy of the Poison Sea

Organic material made up only a fraction of the poison sea shales; clays made up most of the rest. Clays, in large quantities, can be very meaningful to a geologist because they provide the first sign that a distant mountain building event has begun. Clays are lightweight materials. A grain of clay, once lofted into the currents, can travel an extremely long distance, perhaps hundreds of miles. It is much the same for silt, grains of which are only a little larger than those of clay. The weathering and erosion of a landscape can produce and scatter a considerable amount of clay and silt, collectively called mud. Mud travels by way of marine currents, which will eventually be in an offshore direction. Transport continues until those currents grow too slow to carry their burden. The clays then settle lightly and slowly to the sea floor and, along with organic matter, accumulate as muds. With the weight of burial the muds are squeezed into very thinly laminated, dark-colored rocks called shales.

Many of the earliest and oldest Catskill shales are jet black, and they form the lower levels of what is called the **Marcellus Group.** As we have seen, they are the record of the Catskill poison seas. The poison sea beds are immediately overlain by the middle and upper beds of the Marcellus Group, similar looking but very different deposits. These are fossiliferous black shales and dark gray sandstones. They have a sometimes rich assemblage of brachiopods, clams and even corals (Chapter Seven). These were mud-bottomed seas, but they were deposited at times when there was a fairly large amount of oxygen in those waters, at least enough to allow marine shellfish to survive and even flourish. These can be fun rocks to poke through, for they are occasionally richly fossiliferous and the preservation of those fossils can be very good.

Field Trips to the Poison Sea

The shiny, jet-black shales, which are produced in the poison seas, are easily identified. They usually contain few or no fossils, and the few fossils in them are of planktonic shellfish. You will see such rocks sometimes in the lower Schoharie Creek valley above Middleburgh and along Rt. 20, north and northeast of Cherry Valley. Look for the jet-black outcrops. One can be seen about half a mile west of the Rt. 166 intersection, but the best one is 2.6 miles east of it (figure 4-1). At that location you can see two horizons of the Marcellus black shales separated by the Cherry Valley Limestone. If you examine the shales, note the very thin lamination of the rocks (figure 4-2). You may find an occasional small fossil clam and abundant, very small conical fossils called styliolinids (figure 7-23). The Cherry Valley Limestone is the last of the real limestones in this vicinity; although you can find corals and nautiloids (Chapter Seven) in it, collecting specimens is nearly impossible in that dense limestone.

The poison sea deposits are overlain by fossiliferous dark shales and sandstones. To see these in abundance, the best place to visit is the Hudson Valley. Not only are these strata common in that area, but there is even a small mountain range composed of these rocks. It's called the Hoogeberg Range, the most prominent mountain of which is Mt. Marion, located west of Saugerties.

Not surprisingly, the strata of this area are called the Mt. **Marion Formation**. It displays a large number of thinly-bedded, shiny black shales that appear to be the last deposits of the poison sea. Many of the other beds are fossiliferous sandstones and shales and they can be enjoyable to look through. The very best exposure is along Rt. 209, south of Sawkill. There, a massive cliff of black strata towers above the road on both sides. With careful hunting, I found fossil corals and brachiopods. Another fine location can be found by taking the Glasco Turnpike about a half mile west from Rt. 31 to where it crosses Plattekill Creek. There, another large cliff towers above the creek. This location has yielded dozens of species of brachiopods, clams and other fossils (Chapter Seven).

Figure 4-1: Black shales along Rt. 20.

Figure 4-2: Close-up of black shales.

Clearing of the Poison Sea

There is a recognizable history in the black sedimentary strata of the Hudson Valley. The darkest beds of the poison sea are found at the bottom of the sequence. They are jet-black and thinly laminated, with very few or almost no fossils. Upwards, the strata become thicker-bedded, lighter-colored, and fossiliferous. Then the shales are joined by thick ledges of dark sandstone. Finally, at the top of the Mt. Marion Formation, the sequence is mostly dark gray sandstone. It's these heavy, sturdy ledges that make up the top of the Hoogeberg Range. You can see them at the top of Mt. Marion from the Hudson Valley below.

The sequence records a shift from deep-water, oxygen-poor, stagnant seas to shallower, agitated, oxygen-rich waters. The sequence is one of a shallowing ocean, and that is an example of a marine regression. (Earlier, we saw its opposite, a marine transgression.) As the regression continued, more and more sands were pouring into the sea. In fact, it appears that the sands were even filling up the old poison sea. Clearly, something big was happening—but what was it?

**Figure 4-3: Mt. Marion Formation, intersection of
Glasco Turnpike and Plattekill Creek.
Shallowing environments toward the top.**
Courtesy New York State Museum.

Chapter Five

Mountains On Top of Mountains

IT was 2,300 years ago that Plato wrote of a great island, "larger than Libya and Asia taken together." His island was the fabled Atlantis, and it lay out in the Atlantic Ocean beyond the Straits of Gibraltar. The story went on: Fully 9,000 years before Plato's time, Atlantis had been a great city state which controlled an empire extending as far east as Egypt and Italy. Its glory would not last. After losing a war with Athens, Atlantis was consumed by a day-and-a-half of earthquakes and floods. The whole land mass sank into the ocean and has been lost ever since.

It's a wonderful story and just the type that we scientists love to debunk. But the word "debunk" implies ridicule, and when you ridicule a popular myth, you run the risk of appearing arrogant. Now, believe me, arrogance is not exactly unheard of in science, so let's take a careful look at the story of Atlantis. The true story, as is so often the case, is a lot better than the myth.

You can start by climbing the Escarpment Trail on the Catskill Front. You must climb past many ledges in a thick sequence of rock. Many geologists have gone this way and have pondered the same question: Where did all this rock come from? There are several thousand feet of sandstone beneath the Catskill Front, and that's only part of what is sometimes called the **"Appalachian sequence."** The whole sequence consists of sedimentary rocks that are approximately 40,000 feet thick. All of this sediment had to come from somewhere, and 40,000 feet of it had to come from somewhere very big, so you can appreciate the geological curiosity.

In the 1840s the great Albany geologist, James Hall, became interested in finding out where all that sand had come from. He traced these sediments across North America and convinced himself that the thick Appalachian deposits always thinned to the west. Thus he concluded that they came from a source in the east. Now James Hall had no interests in the myth of Atlantis, but others wondered about that source land. Was it the real Atlantis?

In the late 19th century, Charles Callaway calculated the total volume of sediment that made up the Appalachian sequence. From these calculations he estimated that there must have once been a source land about the size of Australia out there in the North Atlantic. Callaway reasoned that the weathering and erosion of this source land provided the sediments of the Appalachian sequence and similar rocks in Europe. Consequently, Callaway thought that he had come up with the scientific discovery of an ancient lost continent—a real one! He called it "Old Atlantis." Old indeed: Callaway's continent would have been about 400 million years older than Plato's.

Elements of Callaway's idea remained popular into the early 20th century, but the theory didn't hold up all that well as oceanographers continued to learn more and more about the floor of the North Atlantic. Surely, if there had once been an Atlantis out there, some remnant would remain, but none was ever found.

The solution to the source land problem came in the late 1960s and it was a terrific story, much greater than the old myth. We geologists know it as our theory of **plate tectonics**. Continents and oceans, it turned out, were not eternal, and even the Atlantic Ocean had not always been there. Neither had North America or Europe; instead there were great land masses, ancestral to the ones we know today. Back then, an ancestral Europe was drifting westward and actively colliding with an earlier form of North America. As the two crushed together, a great mountain range was upthrust all along the collision zone. Such things still happen today. India is colliding with Asia and the Himalayas are the product of that collision. It was not Atlantis, but our 400-million-year-old ancestral Appalachians (called the Acadian Mountains) that actually provided the sediments we see today in places like the Catskill Front.

So the Atlantis of Plato's myth never did exist. But it's not arrogance when we debunk his story; rather it's confidence that science can provide a better story. Our story tells of moving and colliding continents and speaks of once-towering mountain ranges which are no more. It's a good story and one of the most important scientific discoveries of the 20th century. And to me, the best part is that the story comes from reading the rocks.

Plate Tectonics

The story of plate tectonics began with the curiosity of a German meteorologist named Alfred Wegener. There was nothing original in Wegener's observations. Many people had noticed the same thing: There is an apparent fit between the continents of the world. The western coasts of Europe and Africa, for example, fit quite well to the eastern coasts of North and South America. The four continents and Greenland fit together like five giant jigsaw puzzle pieces.

What made Wegener original was that he developed this observation into his theory of **continental drift**. Wegener argued that the continents of the world are mobile and that they move or drift across the surface of the globe. Sometimes they drift apart and open up oceans in between. That accounts for the Atlantic and the similarity of its eastern and western shores. Continents, he argued, could also collide with each other.

Wegener was on the right track, but his theory eventually proved inadequate to describe all of the phenomena which are associated with the movement of continents. We now have replaced his theory of continental drift with the modern-day theory of plate tectonics.

Understanding the nature of plate tectonics and mountain-building is important in our story, but the theory of plate tectonics is a recent one. When I was a student, plate tectonics had just been born and it had not spread to all the geology classes of the time. Since then, I've seen plate tectonics become a cornerstone of geology and it has permeated every branch of the science, including the history of the Catskills.

Plate tectonics is the theory which explains much of the dynamics of the earth's crust. The theory is based upon the observation that the earth's crust is divided into about 20 giant jigsaw puzzle-like pieces called **plates**. All of these plates have a lower layer composed of a black, fine-grained rock called basalt. You may have seen basalt; the Palisades of the lower Hudson River are composed of it. So are the Holyoke and Watchung ranges of Connecticut and New Jersey. Some crustal plates contain an upper horizon composed of granite. This is a familiar stone in graveyards. These are the continents. All plates are mobile and constantly colliding with, or diverging from, their neighbors. These motions, the collisions in particular, greatly affect the surface of the Earth as they result in mountain-building episodes. That's what happened in the Catskill vicinity long ago.

Early Catskill Crustal History

Let's go back a little more than 400 million years to a time called the Silurian period and learn about geological plates and their distributions at that time (figure 5-1A). North America, then the major regional plate, was a mass of granite overlying a thick horizon of basalt. The North American continent was different then; this granitic continent was much smaller and, unlike today, most of the continent was submerged beneath shallow seas. The Catskill vicinity lay on the western edge of a large peninsula that made up the earliest manifestation of the Appalachian Mountain Range. The Appalachian Basin, a crustal depression, lay to the west of this peninsula. It was occupied by relatively shallow seas. The whole region was also located well within the equatorial latitudes at that time.

A conventional deep-water ocean lay to the east, but not our familiar Atlantic Ocean; that ocean did not yet exist. Mind you, the water was there, but the Atlantic Ocean basin had not yet formed. Instead, east of the Catskills, was the western **Iapetus Sea** (figure 5-1A). While the North American plate was composed

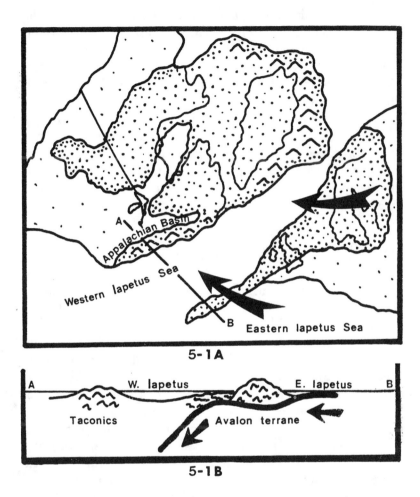

5-1A

5-1B

Figure 5-1A: Map of Western Hemisphere during the Late Silurian. Heavy stippling for land; light stippling for shallow seas. Baltica with its southern extension, the Avalon terrane, approaches North America from the east. The western Iapetus Sea is squeezed in between. The eastern edge of North America is fringed by the old Taconic Mountains and, west of them, the Appalachian Basin.

Figure 5-1B: A cross-section view along line A-B. Arrows show crustal dynamics. There is considerable disagreement about the exact nature of this structure, and this represents one of several possibilities.

mostly of granite, the Iapetus sea floor was underlain by the denser, darker basalt. The Iapetus Sea was bisected by the **Avalon terrane**, a mountainous landscape (figure 5-1A). Beyond that was the eastern Iapetus Sea and then the next granite continent, Europe, then called **Baltica**. Much of Baltica was also submerged by shallow seas.

To the south was the African plate. It would eventually advance toward—and collide with—North America, but not until long after our story is over. This account of the origins of the Catskill Mountains is primarily about the North American Plate and its collision with the Avalon portion of the European plate.

The Devonian Period

The story of the Catskills is, as we have already seen, the story of the Devonian time period. It and the Silurian ranged from about 450 to 360 million years ago.

The Devonian Period was named during the 1830s for units of rocks in the area of Devonshire, England. There, geologists found a distinctive sequence of red sandstones which they called **"Old Red Sandstone."** That unit contains a lot of fossil invertebrates, fish and plants.

By the late 1830s, the New York State Geological Survey was established and its pioneer scientists were busy studying the geology of our state. When the state geologists completed their first survey of the Catskill vicinity, they found a sequence of rocks very similar to that found in the English Devonian. They recognized the similarities and were the first to make a trans-oceanic **"correlation."** That is, they were the first to establish time links between two similar rock units on separate continents. The Old Red Sandstone and the Catskill sequence were essentially the same, even though they were on separate continents.

Nowadays, we geologists do that sort of correlation all the time. Any experienced geologist can quickly recognize a fossil-rich Devonian sequence anywhere in the world on the basis of its distinctive fossils. But in the 1830s this type of correlation was a great step forward for the science of geology.

It must have been puzzling, though, for geologists to recognize that rocks on different continents could be so similar. They probably did not fully appreciate, as we do now, what a fine example of the Devonian Period our New York State section was. These Devonian strata make up nearly all of the southern tier of New York State from the Hudson River to Lake Erie. They make up a thick sequence of rocks recording a wide variety of ancient environments across an impressive expanse of ancient geography. If you are interested in Devonian geology, then New York State is certainly worth the trip.

The Acadian Orogeny

At the dawn of the Devonian Period, the Catskills did not yet exist. The Catskill vicinity, along with western New England, was recovering from an earlier mountain-building event called the **Taconic Orogeny** ("orogeny" means "mountain genesis"). The Taconic Mountains of western New England had nearly eroded away (figure 5-1B). Nearby shallow seas stretched across North America from the Taconics to the western edge of the continent (figure 5-1A).

To the east of the future Catskills, the continent of Baltica was moving westward (figure 5-1A). Stretching southward from Baltica was that thinner slice of land, the Avalon terrane. It, too, was moving toward North America. A major continental collision was soon to occur.

It's hard to tell exactly when a mountain-building event begins; such things are gradual. But a number of events occurring in the early Devonian which heralded the onset of mountain building. One was the gradual deepening of the Appalachian Basin. It's a curious thing but commonly the case that, as mountain ranges begin to rise, the adjacent crust often subsides, forming a basin (figure 5-2B). Tall mountain ranges are thus often parallel to deep marine basins. The early Devonian seas invaded the subsiding Appalachian Basin and they would eventually stretch from the Maritime provinces of Canada to Alabama. The water depths were very shallow at first; these were the waters of the Helderberg Sea, a stage in the development of the Appalachian Basin. As we have seen, this sea accumulated the kind of soft, pink and white sands that harden into limestones.

Such shallow tropical limestone seas are typical of quiet periods of crustal stability, times that immediately precede the onset of real mountain-building. All that was soon to end, however. The Iapetus Sea was closing as both Baltica and the Avalon terrane approached from the east. The collision began in the north as Baltica closed upon Greenland and the Canadian Maritime provinces. Then, like a scissors closing, Baltica, rotating clockwise upon New England and the Avalon terrane, joined in to complete the collision (figure 5-2A). The result was the Acadian Orogeny. First there was a slow collision and then, since there was nowhere else for crustal materials to go, a gradual upward swelling of the crust ensued (figure 5-2B). That's mountain-building. Uplift was gradual at first, and then it speeded up and continued, probably for several tens of millions of years, sometimes rapidly, sometimes slowly. Before it was even half over the Acadian mountain-building event had produced an enormous range of mountains stretching from northern Greenland to someplace south of New York State; these were the Acadians, at their zenith.

These mountains are virtually all gone; only the Berkshires remain as a faint reminder of what was once there. However, whenever I stand on the edge of the Catskill escarpment and gaze eastward, I can well imagine the profile of these mountains rising before me (figure 5-3). It is something to imagine.

The Catskill Delta

The dynamics of all of this crustal activity are quite predictable. The mountains rose and began to weather and erode; the Appalachian Basin began to subside and receive sediment from the nearby mountains. In the economy of nature, erosion in the uplifted mountains led to deposition in the adjacent subsiding

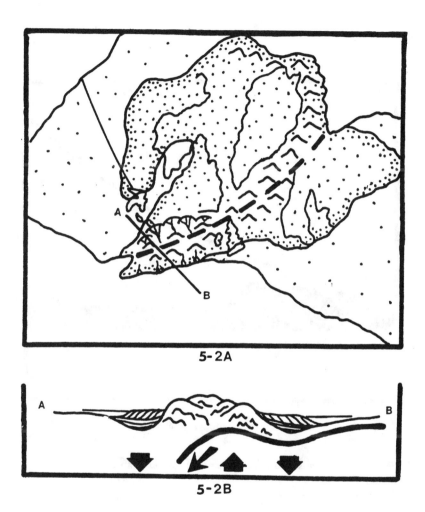

5-2A

5-2B

Figure 5-2A: Map of Western Hemisphere during the Devonian Acadian Orogeny. Heavy stippling for land; light stippling for shallow seas. Baltica has collided with North America, causing the uplift of the Acadian Mountains.

Figure 5-2B: Cross-sectional view along line A-B. The rising Acadian Mountains are shedding sediment into adjacent basins. Arrows show crustal dynamics.

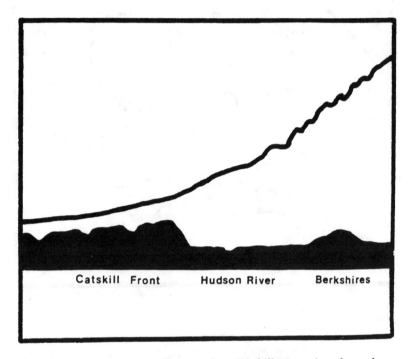

Figure 5-3: A cross-section of the modern Catskills. Looming above them is the profile of the ancient Acadian Mountains, forebears of the Catskills.

Figure 5-4: Cross-sections of the eastern Catskills and western Hudson Valley showing structure of sedimentary rocks. Highly distorted rocks at lower right were deformed by the Taconic Orogeny.

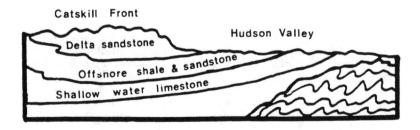

basin (figure 5-2B). Two major masses of rock were deposited upon the early Devonian limestones. These were, first, the off-shore marine shales and sandstones of the Appalachian Basin, and second, the terrestrial deposits of the great **Catskill delta complex** (figure 5-4). In fact, both masses can be viewed as part of the delta complex. It's time to learn about that delta.

In one area of today's world there is an event going on that is roughly analogous to the Acadian Mountain-building event; that is in the Himalayan uplift. The Himalayas are the product of a collision between India and Asia, a collision which has been under way for several tens of millions of years now. The Acadians may or may not have been as tall as the Himalayas, but otherwise the histories of these two mountain ranges are quite similar.

The Himalayas, like the ancient Acadians, have been weathering, eroding and shedding sediment ever since their first uplift. These sediments are transported downstream and into the ocean or, in this case, the Bay of Bengal. Over the many millions of years that this has been going on, the great Ganges Delta has been constructed by the major rivers draining the Himalayan slopes. The delta has been accumulating sediment and expanding into the Bay of Bengal all this time.

The best way I can think of to illustrate the dynamics of the growth of these modern and ancient delta complexes is to look at a convenience store recently built near Oneonta (figure 5-5). This store was built on property where there was a steep slope descending from the road to the floor of the adjacent valley. Because there was not enough flat land for the construction, fill was brought in and dumped. Then a bulldozer plowed the fill into a flat platform big enough for the convenience store and its parking lot.

Take a look at the result. The flat surface is the product of the bulldozer, but the slope beyond it is the product of gravity. The slope is steep; we call that the **angle of repose**. It is the steepest slope that is stable under normal conditions. Beyond this slope is the normal valley floor, which is nearly flat.

Now look at figure 5-6. This is the typical profile of a delta. The upper flat surface is called the **topset**. It is made up of river deposits, usually sands, which were swept into a flat surface by river currents, much as the bulldozer created a flat surface. Beyond the topset is the **foreset**. Here sediments are deposited on an inclined surface that dips seaward at an angle of repose. Again, as at the convenience store, gravity has pulled this material downhill into a stable slope. Under water, the angle of repose is far less steep than on land. Beyond the foreset is the delta **bottomset**. These are the deposits that reach the open ocean sea floor.

Figure 5-5: A convenience store near Oneonta, built on bulldozed fill.

What we learn from the convenience store analogy is the depositional dynamics of the delta. Whether it be bulldozer or river current, a delta creates a flat-lying sedimentary platform. Beyond that, gravity takes over and creates a slope. That's how the basic form of the small delta or the larger delta complex comes into existence.

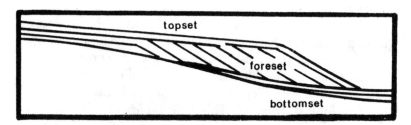

Figure 5-6: Cross sectional view showing structure of a delta.

We still need to understand something about the elevation of the topset, or actually the absence of elevation. The topset has two parts; the offshore part is submerged under only a little water, while the onshore half is emergent, but only a little bit above sea level. This is because the onshore portion is constantly swept by flood currents. Any river deposits that might have been piled up much above sea level will be leveled off by the currents of the next floodwaters. Offshore deposition piles up sediment to about the low-tide mark and then any new sediments are simply carried farther offshore. So, on land, river currents spread out sediments at sea level while, at sea, marine currents deposit sediments up to sea level. In the end there is very little relief on a delta topset.

If you are at all knowledgeable about places like the lower Mississippi Valley or the Ganges Delta of Bangladesh, then you will be comfortable with the image that I have created for the Catskill delta complex. Both of these locations, just barely above sea level, are nearly flat plains. The main stream of such rivers tends to split and split again. We say that the main stream breaks up into many **distributaries** and these streams distribute the waters into the ocean (figure 5-7). Drainage is good where the

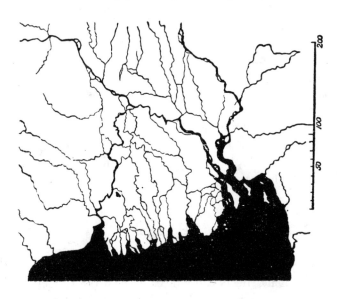

Figure 5-7: Distributary streams of the Ganges Delta.

main river channels empty into the ocean, but elsewhere drainage is poor. There are many swamps and ponds. There are also many small, often sluggish streams; all of the smaller distributaries are likely to be sluggish. Any good map of the lower Mississippi or Ganges rivers will display this very well. Again, here is uniformitarianism in action.

Delta growth continues as long as there are mountains upstream that are weathering, eroding and serving as source lands for sediment to be carried downstream and onto the delta. In the case of the Mississippi, that is going to be a very long time, for the eastern Rocky Mountains and even the western Appalachians are very sizable source lands. In the case of the Ganges Delta, that is going to be an enormous length of time, indeed, probably tens of millions of years, I should think. The Himalayas are big and will not erode quickly. Similar lengths of time apply to the Catskill delta complex, but that was about 400 million years ago and erosion and deposition were long ago completed.

That's it—the origin of the Catskill rocks in a nutshell. Early on, a plate collision began to produce the Appalachian Basin and the Acadian Mountains. Then, erosion of the mountains led to deposition, which began to fill in the basin. First there was the limestone-producing Helderberg Sea. Then came the black muds of the poison sea. We have seen these already, but now we understand them in a broader context. Finally, these basins were filled in and buried by the mud and sand of the advancing Catskill Delta. It's the delta deposits that make up most of what we see in the Catskills today. We will learn about them in the following chapters. If you follow the last several pages, then you are off to a good start in truly understanding the origins of the Catskills. If not, take a good look at the pictures of this chapter again; they tell most of the story.

Field Trips

You cannot go out and see the Acadian Orogeny; it's over. But some of its effects can still be seen in the Catskills. From Windham, travel east on Rt. 23 down toward the town of

Figure 5-8: Tightly folded rocks of the Acadian Orogeny.

Figure 5-9: Slickensides. This may seem like a poor picture, but if you get to see the real thing, you will see that it looks very much like this.

Catskill. You will cross Catskill Creek and then the New York State Thruway. Just past the Thruway you will enter a stretch of highway with steep cliffs of the Helderberg Limestone. The strata of this vicinity were deformed, sometimes intensely (figure 5-8), during the Acadian Mountain-building event. This deformation occurred deep within the crust, but erosion has brought these structures to the surface. See how the strata are steeply inclined and folded. If you have never seen rock structure like this before, you may be surprised at how much seemingly hard and brittle rock can be deformed.

Turn onto County Road 145, and you will soon see some very steeply dipping units of rocks along the road. The surfaces of these strata display fine striations that are called **slickensides** (figure 5-9). These record the movement of the rock masses along fault planes during deformation. Park your car safely somewhere and wander the area's outcrops. Stay away from traffic. Along with the Acadian structures, there is good fossil hunting here.

You can also see some more fine examples of deformed strata along Rt. 9W, south of Saugerties. There the Helderberg Limestone forms sturdy ledges that dip steeply toward the road (figure 5-10). As you travel around this part of the Hudson Valley, you will find many exposures of rock that were deformed in a similar manner.

Figure 5-10: Tilted strata of the Acadian Orogeny.
On Rt. 9W, south of Saugerties.

Chapter Six

The Hamilton Sea

A T the top of the Mt. Marion Formation there is an important change in the rock types. The black shales, which had been so characteristic of the Appalachian Basin, came to be replaced by thick beds of dark sandstones. They make up the crest of Mount Marion itself. You can see great ledges of these strata from the valley below.

Above and beyond those dark sandstones is a sequence of brown shales and fine-grained, brown sandstones, which is sometimes rich in the fossils of marine shellfish. These are the first deposits of what I will call in this book "the Hamilton Sea." The rocks, formally known as the Hamilton Group, are named after the town where Colgate University is located. The brown sandstones of the Hamilton are not well developed in the Hudson Valley. They can be seen at a few locations around the community of Ruby and also along nearby John Carle Road. These rocks are thickest and best exposed in the Schoharie Creek Valley and to the west across all of New York State.

Two key changes occurred in the Hamilton Sea. One was the increased abundance of oxygen. Where the sea floor was current-swept, it was usually well oxygenated. Little organic matter can be preserved in such a setting; most of it decays. That's why the sediments are usually some shade of gray or brown instead of black.

Where the waters were oxygenated, they were often inhabited by large populations of marine invertebrates. The results are sedimentary rocks which are fossiliferous, and these shales and

Figure 6-1: Bedding and water depth. *Top left:* **Thinly laminated, fine-grained shale associated with very deep, quiet-water conditions.** *Top right:* **Thicker-bedded strata from a shallower, more agitated sea floor.** *Lower left:* **A thicker-bedded, more blocky, fine-grained sandstone from still shallower sea floor.** *Lower right:* **Thick-bedded, blocky, course-grained sandstone associated with shallowest, current-swept conditions.**

sandstones have some of the best fossil hunting anywhere in the Devonian sequence. The Hamilton fossils are often abundant, diverse, and a lot of fun to hunt.

The second key change was the increased rate of deposition. The Hamilton Sea accumulated great thicknesses of sediment, mostly mud and sand that poured off the rising Acadian Mountains. Thus, with the Hamilton sandstones, we have clear evidence that the Acadian mountain-building event, which had begun in Helderberg times, was at last fully under way.

Environments

But before visiting the Hamilton, let's first learn about the environments that shales and sandstones were deposited in. These were ancient seas, but what else can we deduce about them? What about water depth? Today, that's easy to determine; any sea, no matter how deep, can be plumbed with depth-sounding equipment. But what about an ancient sea? It would seem that water depth would be impossible to determine, and it usually is. But occasionally it is possible.

Let me introduce you to the basics of how a field geologist "guesstimates" the depth of ancient seas. I have put together a series of photos of strata which I believe came from progressively shallower waters (figure 6-1). The first shows a very thinly laminated shale. It *probably* came from deep water. How deep? I don't know, but it had to be deep enough so that the water currents were near zero, and only very thin sheets of very fine clay could accumulate. That is what makes a shale.

The succeeding photos show a spectrum of stratified rock that probably formed in progressively more agitated and probably shallower waters. Agitated waters carry and deposit much more sediment. With increasing current agitation, the stratified beds become progressively thicker, and the rocks are steadily lighter in color. You probably cannot tell this from the photos, but the beds grade from materials which are mostly silt and clay to beds which are mostly sand; in short from shales to sandstones, from deep to shallow.

If you spend enough time looking at marine sedimentary rocks, you will become comfortable recognizing this gradation of lithologies. However, rocks will often lie to you. Thinly laminated shales can form in a mud puddle, and that's not the bottom of a deep sea! Similarly, thickly-bedded sandstones can sometimes form in a deep basin, which is not shallow water. But, more often than not, rocks do tell the truth. At least they always tell you which way to bet. A word of caution is needed, however. These deductions apply only to the marine deposits. Later, when we get to the rocks of the Catskill Delta, there are different things to watch for and water depth is of no significance.

In attempting to deduce ancient water depths, we can go by other criteria. They are the **physical primary structures**. These are sculpted into the soft sediments by currents. They include structures such as **ripple marks** (figure 8-6 and 8-14), delicate ripples of sand sculpted by passing waves and currents. Then there are **cross beds** (arrow, figure 6-2). Here, shifting currents deposit sediment on inclined surfaces, first one way and then, often, another. Advancing submarine dunes can also produce cross beds. Sometimes submarine currents scour out **troughs** in

**Figure 6-2: Arrow points to cross bedding in the Hamilton Group.
Schoharie Creek Valley.**

Figure 6-3: Arrow points to base of channel form in the
Hamilton Group. Schoharie Creek Valley.

the sea floor. When these are filled in with sediment, the result is
called **trough cross bedding**. In a few instances, I have seen
extreme examples of this where large channel cross-sections have
been scoured out of the Hamilton Sea floor (figure 6-3).

One final type of primary structure is the **shell lag deposit**.
Watch for three- or four-inch-thick beds composed of a hash of
whole and broken shells, mostly brachiopods. These were left
behind when strong currents swept the sea floor, carried off all
the fine-grained sediment and left the shells behind. All these are
most typical of shallow, current-swept sea floors.

With that brief background we can take a look at the Hamilton strata and make some elementary deductions about water
depths. What we see are mostly thin-bedded shales. That suggests
quiet and deep-water conditions. These were deposited in water
that was below what we call **fair weather wave base**, which is to
say that the sea floor was deep enough to lie undisturbed except
during major storms. The shales are sometimes interrupted by
thick sandstone beds, and these have often been interpreted as
representing moments of intense storm-wave activity. Great
storms passed across the sea and stirred up large amounts of sand

and redeposited them. The storm beds often display ripple marks and cross beds.

There are other primary structures to watch for in the Hamilton Sea. Among the most enigmatic are those variously called **flow rolls, storm rollers,** or **ball-and-pillow structures** (figure 6-4). These are rounded and folded masses of sandstone, usually lying above shales. While still sand, they appear to have been subjected to some sort of physical disruption, probably gravity-induced, at some time after deposition while they were still soft. We really don't know exactly how they form, however.

Figure 6-4: Flow rolls. Schoharie Creek Valley.

While you and I would consider the Hamilton Sea deep, that's not exactly true. The Hamilton sandstones and shales were deposited on relatively shallow-water sea floors—shallow, that is, by the standards of most oceans. As we saw, these were often very hospitable sea floors with plenty of oxygen and at least enough current agitation to keep sea-floor conditions from stagnating. Rich invertebrate ecologies often flourished on these sea floors.

Nevertheless, despite the favorable setting, many of the Hamilton sediments are unfossiliferous. Sometimes oxygen content was just a little too low to support shellfish. The dark brown, very thin-bedded shales probably represent such times. At other times the rates of deposition were so rapid that few shellfish could survive; they faced suffocation in the murky, silty waters and avoided such areas. Or, they might have been present, but their skeletal remains were so thinly spaced in the muds that they are, like needles in a haystack, hard to find. We call this **sediment dilution**.

Field Trips to the Hamilton Sea

The deposits of the Hamilton are best exposed in the northwestern Catskills. Look for exposures in the Schoharie Creek Valley, south of Middleburgh and north of Blenheim. Follow County Rt. 31 from North Blenheim to Fultonham, and you will encounter many outcrops. There are more exposures at Vroman's Nose near Middleburgh; all of these are fine exposures, but they yield few fossils. This vicinity was close to the rising Acadian Mountains. So much sediment poured into the area that shellfish remains, if they were here, have become lost in the muds through sediment dilution.

The best places to see the Hamilton Sea are to the west. Follow the Hamilton rocks along a straight line running from Middleburgh to my favorite locations around Lake Otsego. Strata deposited in good deep water ecologies are exposed just above the eastern and western shores of the lake. Those beds are dark, fine-grained, thinly-bedded and only poorly fossiliferous. Look at the increasingly thick-bedded strata at Mohegan Canyon, at Five Mile Point on the west shore, and see evidence of shallowing seas along with better fossil hunting. Many roadside outcrops are found in the hills above the lake. The higher elevations display rocks from generally shallower waters. There are more locations in the Susquehanna River Valley south as far as Goodyear Lake. The Hamilton is even more widespread in western New York State and it continues to be very fossiliferous through the Finger Lakes Region to Lake Erie.

Chapter Seven

Fossils of the Appalachian Basin

NEW YORK STATE has played a genuinely important role in the history of the science of paleontology. That is largely to the credit of the New York State Museum, its geological survey and its great 19th-century state paleontologist, James Hall. Hall began his career in geology as a student at Rensselaer Polytechnic Institute and soon went on to be an early member of the state geological survey. There he spent a career that lasted more than 60 years, devoting all of this time to describing the paleontology of the state. During his long tenure, Hall and a team of outstanding assistants assembled a comprehensive view of the state's rich fossil heritage. The great bulk of this work was done in the Devonian sequence across the state's Southern Tier, from the Hudson River to Lake Erie. His published works are nearly endless, but he is best remembered for the 13 large tomes on New York State paleontology that he produced from 1846 to 1898. There is almost nothing else comparable anywhere, and these revered books remain, to this day, the foundation for all studies of the state's fossils.

With that introduction to this chapter on fossils, it is disappointing to have to say that throughout most of the Catskills fossil hunting is not very good. A paleontologist would have to search for a long time before finding a decent fossil skeleton anywhere in the Catskills. Plant fossils are common, but they are usually very poorly preserved. The shells of invertebrates do turn up but, again, these are rare finds. Around the edges of the Catskills hunting, improves dramatically. There are many fine locations where rich assemblages of fossil shellfish abound. These are, of course, within the marine sediments of the Appalachian Basin. Spotty as it is, there is a great deal of rewarding fossil hunting in the Catskills and much worth knowing about its fossils.

I do not intend to give you an encyclopedic description of Catskill paleontology in this chapter; that's not possible. But I will describe and illustrate the more common and representative fossils that can be found. I certainly should be able to acquaint you with all of the major groups of fossils that are present. I will focus on the several major marine habitats that make up Catskill rocks: 1) the Bahamas-like Helderberg Sea; 2) the "poison" Marcellus basin; and 3) the mud-bottomed sea floors of the Hamilton Group.

Major Groups of Fossils

Let's begin with a broad introduction to the major groups of marine organisms that are common in the sedimentary rocks of the Appalachian Basin. I will discuss the most primitive forms first and then the successively more complex types.

The Algae: Algae are probably most familiar as the slimy, green pond scum that becomes quite dense in small, stagnant pools late in August. Such forms rarely enter into the fossil record because there are few ways to preserve them. Some other types of algae, however, can be preserved. The most common forms in the Catskills, the blue-green algae of the Helderberg Sea, grew into sticky sheets along the shores of this sea. This happens today on the coast of the Persian Gulf, so we know a lot about them. The sticky algae accumulate sediment into thin laminations that harden into an easily recognizable rock (figure 7-1 and 3-2) referred to as algal laminites or ribbon limestones (Chapter Three).

Corals: Film and still photos of coral reefs portray some of the most vivid and colorful images of today's seas. Such images are difficult to associate with the Catskills but, as in today's

Figure 7-1: Algal laminites from the Manlius Limestone.

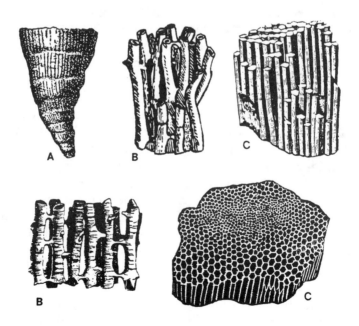

Figure 7-2: Corals. A. horn coral. B. digitate coral. C. honeycomb coral.

tropical seas, corals were sometimes quite common in the old Appalachian Basin. While nothing in the Catskills can match the Great Barrier Reef of Australia, there were some fairly decent reefs in those times. Many of the Devonian forms were **horn corals** (figure 7-2A), so named because they had skeletons shaped like a cow's horn, wide and open at one end and tapering to a point at the other. The chamber within was divided into compartments by walls like you see in a cut-open orange. Other types are called **digitate corals** (figure 7-2B); they grew long, slender branches similar to fingers. A third common group, the **honeycomb corals**, grew massive honeycomb-like skeletons (figure 7-2C) that are similar to the modern-day corals. Corals are only occasionally found throughout the strata of the Appalachian Basin, but they are quite common in the Onondaga Limestone.

Stromatoporoids: The stromatoporoid is a peculiar fossil, intermediate in appearance between the algal laminites and the massive reef corals (figure 7-3). They weren't algae, but like the algae they did grow laminated colonies. They were colonial, reef-building animals, however, much like the corals. They appear to be entirely extinct, so we know nothing of their soft anatomy, and we will thus never be sure what they were. They grew abundantly in the very shallow, near-shore environments of the Manlius Limestone and are seen within that unit, especially to the east as at John Boyd Thacher State Park (see Chapter Two).

Brachiopods: Brachiopods are enormously abundant fossil shellfish. Back in the Devonian they were as common as the clams are today. Like clams, they had two shells; we say they were bivalves. But brachiopods were not clams; they had completely different anatomies. The group is not extinct, but only a few hundred living species are to be found in nature. Very few of those are seen in the temperate climate belts, and I know of none that are found along the east coast of the United States.

But the fossil record is different. More than 30,000 species of brachiopods are known as fossils, and many of those are in the Appalachian Basin. Look at figure 7-4 for some of the common forms. If you do your fossil hunting in upstate New York you will soon become quite familiar with brachiopods. Watch for abundant and rich assemblages of them.

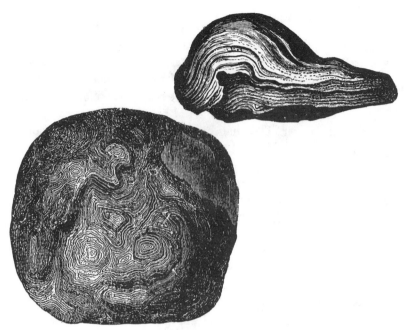

Figure 7-3: Stromatoporoids: This may appear to be a poor drawing, but it is actually quite accurate.

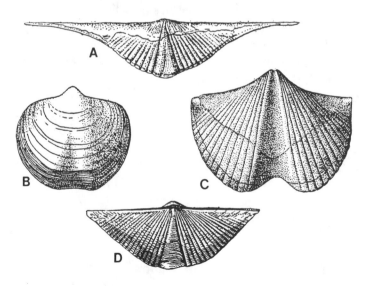

Figure 7-4: Brachiopods. A, C, D. Genus *Spirifer*. B. *Athyris*.
Courtesy New York State Museum.

Figure 7-5: Bryozoan colony.

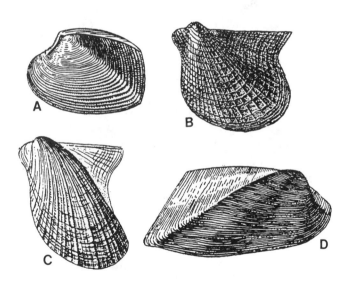

Figure 7-6: Clams: A. *Cypricardella*. B. *Actinopteria*. C. *Pterinea*.
D. *Goniophora*.
Courtesy New York State Museum.

James Hall was fascinated by the brachiopods, and much of his 13 books on New York State paleontology is devoted to their description. He and his colleagues were pioneers in this branch of invertebrate zoology, and they discovered and described hundreds of brachiopod species.

Bryozoa: Closely related to the brachiopods, but very different in appearance, are the bryozoa (figure 7-5). The word bryozoa means "moss animals" and that's about what they look like. (Actually, the word that comes to my mind is "lacy" instead of "mossy.") Anyway, the bryozoa are very delicate colonial animals and many of them live together in colonies that grow on the sea floor or encrust large shells. Their skeletons produce the delicate, lacy network that identifies them. They were never very large and not often common in the Catskills.

Mollusks: Some other fossil groups are so familiar you can hardly tell these ancient shellfish from their modern counterparts. Most of the mollusks, for example, have changed little through time. **Clams** and **snails** are fine examples. Both groups had, by the Devonian time period, evolved much of their modern-day morphology, and many of them are indistinguishable from their modern descendants. Look at figure 7-6 and 7-7. You will find that many of these Devonian mollusks have a remarkably familiar look to them.

A type of mollusk you're not likely to be familiar with is the **cephalopod.** Actually, you are bound to know about some of them, the squids and octopods, but the Devonian ones are different. Squids and octopods are commonly referred to as "naked" cephalopods, simply because they have no shell. The Devonian forms did have shells, and most of them belong to a group called the **nautiloids.** Several of them are illustrated in figure 7-8. The straight shell form is the most primitive type. Nautiloids can be imagined as squid-like creatures living in these chambered, conical shells. More advanced Devonian forms had coiled shells which are also illustrated (figure 7-9). Shelled cephalopods were probably never great swimmers, but the coiled ones were far less clumsy in the water.

Cephalopods, the brightest of the invertebrates, may have evolved their intelligence long ago. During the Devonian they

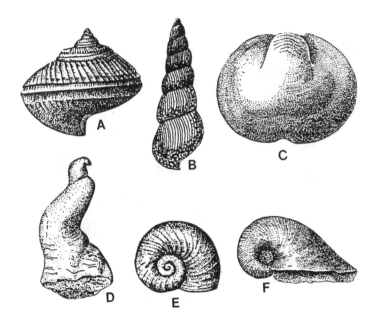

Figure 7-7: Snails: A. *Bembexia*. B. *Loxonema*. C & F. *Ptomatis*
D. *Platyceras*. E. *Diaphorostoma*.
Courtesy New York State Museum.

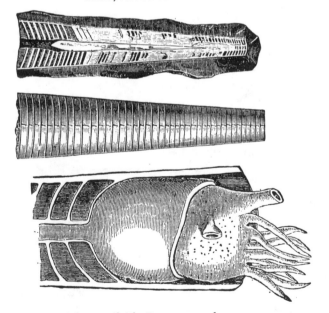

Figure 7-8: Straight nautiloids. Bottom one shows some anatomy.

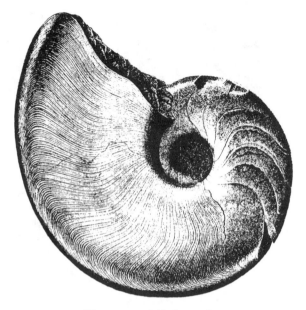

Figure 7-9: Coiled nautiloid.

would have been the smartest forms anywhere. The cephalopods were likely to have been competitors of the fish, because both were predators in the Devonian seas. The fish were better swimmers and by Devonian time they had become the dominant marine predators (Chapter Nine).

Trilobites: Among fossil hunters, the most coveted groups of invertebrate fossils always include the trilobites. The trilobites are arthropods; that means that they have jointed external skeletons that include jointed legs. A good modern example of an arthropod is the lobster. Other modern arthropods include shrimp, crabs, centipedes, millipedes, spiders and, most commonly, insects. All have jointed legs and jointed skeletons. The trilobites are ancient and extinct representatives of this group (figure 7-10). In this introductory book I don't want to use a lot of Latin terminology, but for the trilobites, I think that this is forgivable. The tail of *Dalmanites* is commonly seen in the Helderberg Limestone and the two forms that you should hope to find in the Hamilton beds are *Dipleura* and *Phacops*.

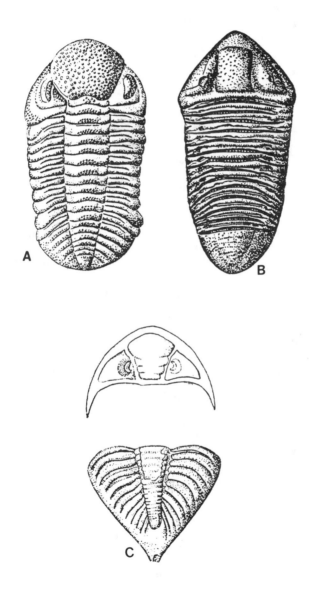

Figure 7-10: Trilobites. A. *Phacops.* **B.** *Dipleura* **C.** *Dalmanites.*
Courtesy New York State Museum.

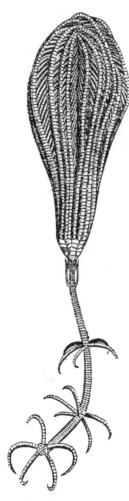

Figure 7-11: Crinoid (sea lily).

Crinoids: Another living, but largely unknown, group of organisms found in the Catskills are the crinoids, also known by their common name, **sea lilies** (figure 7-11). Sea lilies are most remarkable animals. They have five arms, and that clearly indicates their relationship to the starfish. Although five arms is an odd trait for an animal, what makes them truly unusual is their stems; they are stemmed animals! At the base of their stems are root-like structures called holdfasts which tether them to the sea floor. Again, they are animals, but their plant-like morphology is what gives them their common name. Sea lilies grew in "meadows," dense populations of them swaying in the currents (figure 1-2) much as meadow grass sways in the breeze. Today's crinoids are brightly multicolored, adding to their plant-like image. They are especially common in the Coeymans Limestone, although they are rarely well-preserved. Look for abundant scattered stem remains (figure 7-12).

Starfish: Another form that has changed very little since the Devonian is the starfish (figure 7-13). Starfish are rare in the fossil record and that includes the Catskills. However, they do turn up occasionally in the Hamilton Group and the discovery of one makes the fossil hunter's day. The New York State Museum houses a large number of them. One memorable discovery was of 190 specimens on a single bedding plane on Mt. Marion near Saugerties. One of those starfish even seemed to be have been feeding upon a Devonian clam when it was suddenly buried; it remains preserved that way, a truly remarkable fossil!

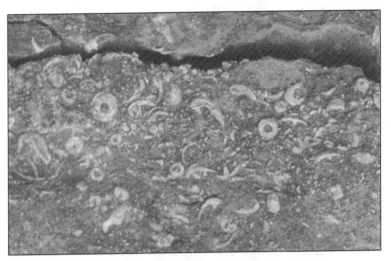

Figure 7-12: Stem remains of crinoids, Coeymans Limestone.

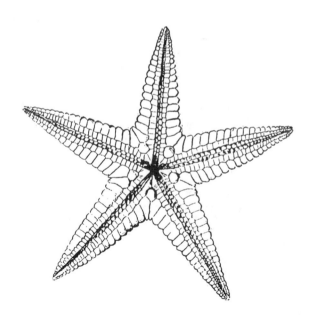

Figure 7-13: Starfish genus *Devonaster*.

Fish: Some Devonian fish are quite familiar-looking, but many of them are bizarre to modern eyes (figure 7-14 and 1-1). Sadly, you are not likely to find a good whole skeleton in or around the Catskills; those are really rare. You might, however, find some isolated bones. The New York State Museum has a good leaflet on Devonian fish, entitled "300 Million Years Ago," and it is free.

There was a diverse and large fauna of fish in the Hamilton Sea, the most abundant of which belonged to a group called the **placoderms**. Placoderms are extinct. To us today, they are a primitive-looking group of fish, but in their time they were a great advance over the most primitive of the fish. They had jaws, something earlier forms lacked (Chapter Nine). A good example is *Bothryolepis* (figure 7-14). This form had a heavily armored front region and a flattened body. It must have been a relatively sluggish swimmer in the Hamilton Sea.

There were some more streamlined placoderms as well. A good example, and one that lived in both the rivers and seas, is *Dinichthys* (figure 7-15). This must have been a very able predator in both the freshwater and marine habitats of the Devonian. Like all other placoderms it didn't have teeth, and that is a primitive trait among fish. Instead it had razor-sharp, meat cleaver-like jaw bones.

As is the case today, Devonian fish occupied the top of the food pyramid; they were the chief predators of the Appalachian Basin. They were not the only predators, however. Very modern-looking sharks shared the seas with the fish. The sharks are almost never found as fossils because they don't have bones and their skeletons are composed of cartilage. Thus, only their teeth are preservable, but I have never seen one in the Catskills. Some forms have been found to the west, a good example of which is *Cladoselache* (figure 7-16).

Nature's oddities: Most fossil hunters are not terribly interested in finding familiar shellfish. What they most want to find are the remains of nature's extinct oddities, fossil forms long lost from this planet. That's part of the fun of fossil hunting: There are so many extinct groups that cannot be properly classified. These are whole lines of evolution which have gone extinct. All

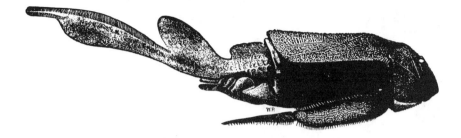

Figure 7-14: Primitive placoderm fish *Bothryolepis*.

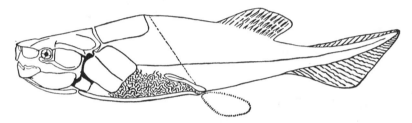

Figure 7-15: Placoderm fish *Dinichthys*.

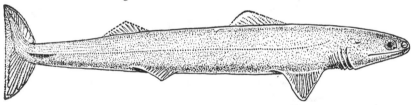

Figure 7-16: Devonian shark *Cladoselache*.

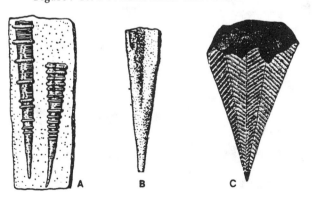

Figure 7-17: A. tentaculitid. B. hyolith. C. conularid.

that is left of them are their skeletons, and that is not always enough to identify them. Although we do not know what they are, we have an abundance of ideas. So let me introduce you to some of the Catskills' less familiar fossil forms.

First is the **tentaculitid** (figure 7-17A). These are small, ridged conical shells. Paleontologists have speculated that these are shell-bearing worms, but this is only a guess. Another mystery form is the **hyolith** (figure 7-17B). Again these are conical shells, but they don't have the ridges of the tentaculitid. What are they? Who knows? They have been extinct for such a long time. A final mystery is the **conularid** (figure 7-17C). These are four-sided, conical forms with chevron ornamentation. While they may be some distant relative of corals and jellyfish, nobody knows for sure. They are quite rare in the Catskills, and I have seen only a few in the Hamilton shales.

Trace fossils: The trace fossil deserves some mention here. All manner of behavior is preserved as trace fossils; although I would enjoy devoting a whole chapter to these marvelous fossils, I can't do that in an introductory book.

Trace fossils are not the remains of an animal's skeleton, but of its activity, such as its footprints. Burrowing activity is the most common type of behavior preserved as a trace fossil. Then there are the trails of animals crawling across the sea floor.

Figure 7-18: Left-to-right dimpled pattern is *Isopodichnus*.

An interesting form, worth looking for all through the marine and non-marine rocks of the Catskills, is a trail called *Isopodichnus* (figure 7-18). We don't know what *Isopodichnus* was, but we guess that it was an arthropod with many legs. Take a look at the figure and see for yourself.

One type of trace fossil you should look for and you will find often is called *Zoophycos* or, commonly, "rooster tails." These are apparently the feeding burrows of marine worms, creatures that dug their way through the sediments, consuming mud as they went. The biological materials of the mud nourished them. Their burrows have a characteristic back-and-forth, horseshoe motion which identifies the form (figure 7-19).

Figure 7-19: Zoophycos.
The animal entered the sediment at the upper left, created back-and-forth, U-shaped burrows and exited at the upper right.
Courtesy New York State Museum.

Hunting Fossils in the Appalachian Basin

Now that we have completed an introduction to the major groups of marine fossils you can look for in the Catskill vicinity, it is time to survey the major rock units of the Appalachian Basin and give you a more specific idea of the fossils to look for when you are in the field.

The Helderberg Sea

When I first explained the Helderberg Sea, I described it as a shallow, tropical, limestone-producing ocean. Imagine shallow, clear, aqua-colored, tropical waters. Then dress up that sea floor with some ancient organisms. Possibly the most common skeletal remains are fragments of the crinoid stems, the columnals as they are called. The sea lilies grew in dense meadows through the lower Helderberg Group, especially in the Coeymans Limestone. Populating the sea floor beneath the meadows were large numbers of brachiopods, clams, bryozoa and trilobites. With death and decay, the various shellfish disarticulated into a hash of skeletal fragments (figure 3-3).

Many other groups of fossils do appear in the Helderberg Sea, but what you find depends on exactly which formation of rock you are looking through. You might review Chapter Three where I described the Cherry Valley vicinity. For corals, visit outcrops of the Onondaga Limestone. They are very common in that unit; in fact much of the lower Onondaga is reef limestone. For delicate fossils, such as the trilobites and bryozoa, visit the Kalkberg Limestone. Its quiet-water sea floor accumulated the remains of these organisms, but usually only as fragments. If you work the Manlius Limestone, watch for the thinly laminated rocks, which are fossil algae mats. Also look for *tentaculitids*. Some of the most common fossil shellfish of the Helderberg Sea are illustrated in figures 7-20 to 7-22.

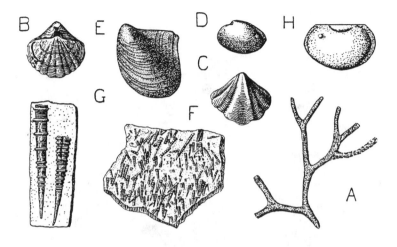

**Figure 7-20: Faunas of the Manlius Limestone. A. bryozoan.
B & C. brachiopods. D & E. clams. F & G. tentaculitids.
H. ostracode, a primitive crustacean.**
Courtesy New York State Museum.

The Poison Sea

The truly poisonous sea deposits have very few fossils in
them. If you are working really thin-bedded and shiny, jet-black
strata, watch for a few small clams and abundant, very small
conical forms called styliolinids (figure 7-23, E & F). These were
planktonic forms; they floated in life and sank to the sea floor
upon death. Few if any creatures actually lived on that sea floor.
Those few dark shale sea floors that were not entirely oxygen-de-
prived did have some sea floor inhabitants, and they did preserve
a number of fossils that are often well preserved but not very
common. Try the large outcrop along Rt. 209 between Sawkill
and Kingston. Do look for brachiopods and horn corals, however.

The Hamilton Sea

As I emphasized earlier, the Hamilton Group is a very
well-known unit of rock, famed for its paleontology. Our image

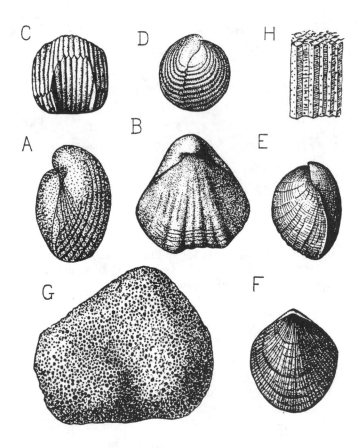

Figure 7-21: Faunas of the Coeymans Limestone. A-F. brachiopods. H & G. corals.

Courtesy New York State Museum.

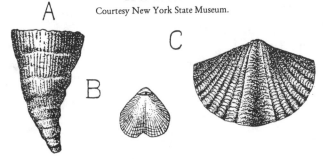

Figure 7-22: Faunas of the Kalkberg Limestone. A. horn coral. B & C. brachiopods.

Courtesy New York State Museum.

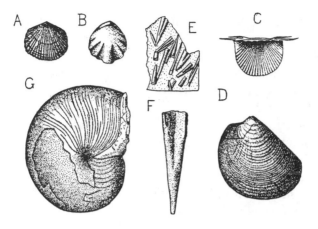

Figure 7-23: Faunas of the poison sea, the Marcellus Group. A-C. brachiopods. D. clam. E. styliolinids. F. hyolith. G. coiled nautiloid.
Courtesy New York State Museum.

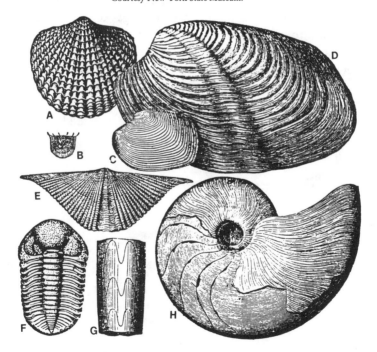

Figure 7-24: Faunas of the Hamilton Group. A, B & E. brachiopods.
C & D. clams. F. trilobite. G. straight nautiloid (fragment).
H. coiled nautiloid.

of the Hamilton Sea floor is not quite as pleasant as it was for the Helderberg Sea. These are not shallow, sunlit and aqua waters. Instead, imagine a deeper, muddy-bottomed setting, largely dark and inhospitable to the human outlook, but not to the invertebrate communities that thrived on the Hamilton Sea floor (figures 7-24 and 7-25).

Look for a bit of everything in the Hamilton. The most common forms by far are the brachiopods; there is an enormous diversity of their shells throughout the Hamilton (figures 7-4 and 7-25). Next in abundance are the clams (figure 7-6), which are nearly as common and diverse. Watch for any number of snails, bryozoa fragments and sometimes segments of crinoid stems. Straight nautiloids are often found, but coiled ones are rare. Trilobite fragments are commonplace, but it takes determined hunting to obtain a good, whole specimen. Don't let that discourage you; they do turn up. The Hamilton can be a fine outdoors museum of Devonian marine paleontology. Of course, not all of the Hamilton is fossiliferous. Much of it was barren sea floor and it is preserved as unfossiliferous shales and sandstone. The best hunting is north and south of Cooperstown, especially in the strata exposed along roads near Lake Otsego. The best luck I have had is in the hills west of and above the lake.

Fossils of the Hamilton Sea can be searched for in the Schoharie Creek Valley as well, although the hunting is more spotty there.

Facing page. Figure 7-25: Faunas of the Hamilton Group.
A & B. brachiopods. C & D. clams. E-G. snails. H. tentaculitid.
I & J. trilobites.
Courtesy New York State Museum.

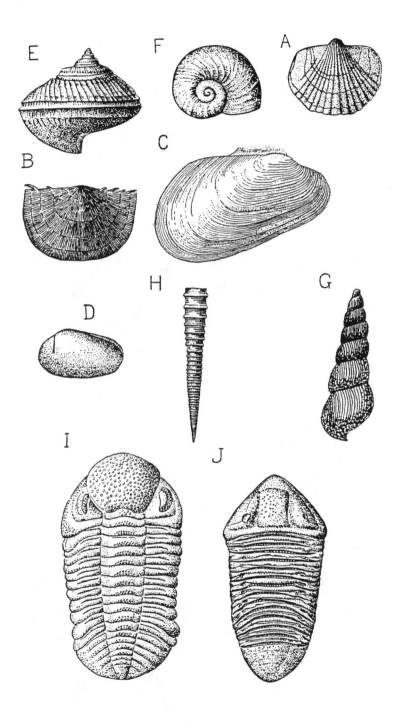

Chapter Eight

A Storied Land

ONE of the most geologically interesting ways for you to enter the Catskills is to take the Glasco Turnpike (Rt. 32) from its intersection with Rt. 9W westward toward Overlook Mountain. Along the way you will pass some fine exposures of the Helderberg and poison seas. About a half mile west of the Kings Turnpike (Rt. 31) you will cross Plattekill Creek (figure 4-3) and soon ascend a hill. Beyond the hill's crest you will enter the true geological realm of the Catskills. From here on, there is a pattern: At close intervals the road approaches rugged ledges of sandstone, rises up and passes over them. On the other side of each ledge the road dips for a short distance. Soon another ledge of sandstone crosses and again the road must pass up and over that one, only to find still another dip.

The process continues as you approach Rt. 212. The Glasco Turnpike ascends one ledge after another; it passes across one dip after another. The ledges are all composed of gray sandstone and the rocks of the softer "dip" beds, although rarely seen, are dark, shaly beds.

At Rt. 212 you have a choice: You can continue straight on the Glasco Turnpike and head toward Overlook Mountain, or, if you would rather, you can take Rt. 212 into Woodstock. It doesn't matter; either way the geology is the same: The ledges of gray sandstone continue, but now the softer beds are composed of red shales.

The pattern here is important. Many rugged sandstone ledges are interbedded with many softer, shaly strata. Catskill stratigraphy is layered like the stories of a tall building. This pattern continues into all of the Catskills, as far west as you care to go.

Patterns are always important. They are nature's way of telling us that there is something that needs to be investigated and understood. And to a scientist that's irresistible. We always leap at the bait and try to understand what it seems that nature wants us to know. Catskill geologists began interpreting this type of pattern many years ago, and that has taken us a long way to really understanding the geological history of the Catskills.

The Catskill Delta Sequence

At last we have reached the main units of Catskill geology: The very rocks which contribute the most to the scenery of our mountains, the brick-red strata of the Catskill Delta. This complex sequence of brown and red shales and sandstones makes up nearly all of the rocks of the mountains themselves. These strata are the direct product of the Acadian mountain-building event described in Chapter Five.

In order to understand these rocks, we have to appreciate that the Catskill Delta was once one of the really big delta complexes of the world, comparable to the Mississippi, Amazon, or, even better, Ganges River deltas. Let's take the Ganges Delta as our model for understanding the Catskill Delta. The parallels are striking. Both are in tropical climates with seasonal monsoon rainfall. But more important, both occupied similar settings adjacent to rising mountain ranges. Earlier we saw that the Catskill Delta was made up of the rivers that drained a rising Acadian mountain range (Chapter Five). This mountain range was produced by the collision of early versions of the North American and European continents. There were quite a few rivers draining the Acadians, each river with its own delta. The many deltas coalesced into the single delta plain we call the Catskill delta complex. Earlier I used a bulldozer analogy to describe how such delta deposition builds up sediments to sea level.

Likewise, the Himalayas are a rising range produced by the collision of land masses—India and the rest of Asia. Two major rivers, the Brahmaputra and the Ganges, deposit delta materials which make up the single delta plain we call the Ganges Delta. The Ganges plain is nearly at sea-level and it's quite flat. A complex equilibrium maintains this sea level elevation; it is not just an accident. Again the bulldozer analogy applies here: A considerable amount of sediment is transported toward the sea, and much of it gets spread out as topset deposits across the delta plain by flood events. But to understand this flat delta plain fully, you need to realize that another major process is occurring here. The whole mass of a large delta is so enormously heavy that it presses into the crust beneath it. The effect is that the whole delta appears to be constantly subsiding. As it subsides, the river brings new topset deposits and spreads them out across the delta plain. These two processes combine to maintain the delta exactly at sea level. Subsidence creates space that deposition fills in with sediment.

This has happened to all of the big deltas around the world and throughout history. It's a major inconvenience where cities are built on such subsiding deltas. New Orleans, for example, was established several hundred years ago, and it has had enough time to begin subsiding beneath sea level, which has happened to more than half of the city. There is no way to stop this and, indeed, the problem will only get worse as New Orleans continues to subside.

The Meandering Streams

The nature of the Ganges River and its deposits varies with the season. Throughout most of the year such rivers are relatively peaceful and their channels are easily large enough to carry their low and moderate flows of clear water. At such times, the rivers meander back and forth through sinuous turns we call **meander loops** (figure 8-1). It is important to understand something of the geometry of the meandering stream. The deepest part of the stream is on the outside edge of its meander. That is also the fastest-flowing part. In general the current speeds decline toward the opposite bank, and, in that direction, the water usually shallows. Centrifugal force carries the currents up against the deep outside edge of the channel and those outside loops are erosive. Quieter waters, on the shallow inside of the loop, are depositional. In the economy of nature, erosion on one side of the river is balanced by deposition on the other.

Figure 8-1: River meander loop, the Schoharie Creek below Vromans Nose.

In the channel itself there is no balance; there sediment inexorably and slowly migrates downstream. Its distant goal is the sea. As the river sediments migrate downstream, they form several types of deposits. The structures of the sediments vary with where they are found in the channel, and these can be recognized in the rocks of the Catskills.

Let's look at some photos from the Catskills. Figure 8-2 shows the sharp boundary between a river sandstone and the underlying shales. This is an erosive surface that formed when the deep, fast-flowing side of a stream cut into the fine-grained sediments and red soils of the floodplain. Coarse-grained gravels can often be found just above the erosion surface. These are pebbles, eroded free from the bank above. Figure 8-3 shows the deposits of the deepest and fastest flowing part of the stream

Figure 8-2: Erosional surface at the base of a Devonian river channel. River sandstone above and red shales below.

Figure 8-3: Trough cross beds.

Figure 8-4: Sheet laminations.

Figure 8-5: Planar cross beds.

channel. Notice how all of the strata are inclined and how different sets of strata cross each other. This structure is called **trough cross bedding**. Trough cross bedded sandstones are the thickest and most commonly seen deposits of the ancient Catskill river channels. They record the downstream motion of small-scale sand "dunes," driven by river currents during high flow periods.

The next several types of river deposits are often found in the middle part of the channel in slightly slower currents. Figure 8-4 shows **sheet laminated beds**. These are thin sheets of sandstones that were laid down under still relatively fast-flowing, midstream currents. Figure 8-5 shows **planar cross bedding**. These beds record the movement of small sand waves in a downstream direction. The next figure shows **ripple marks** (figure 8-6) that form from relatively slow moving currents. The river channel deposits are likely to be associated with thinly laminated, red shales and fine-grained, red sandstone. These are the deposits of the river's floodplain. They are flood deposits and floodplain soils. I will say more on them later.

Occasionally the river banks of our ancient Catskill streams can be recognized. Such river banks are made up of thick-bedded sandstones plastered onto the river shorelines. The sands are often rich in fossil plant debris and sometimes iron stained to a rusty

Figure 8-6. Ripple marks.

Figure 8-7: An ancient river bank. The bank deposits dip and thin out to the left. The massive sandstone above is the river channel deposit.

yellow and brown. These strata are all inclined in the same direction, sloping toward the old river channel. See figure 8-7 for an illustration.

It is curious how ancient and modern histories sometimes interplay. Pratt Rock, just east of Prattsville, was to be Zadock

Figure 8-8: Pratt Rock. Colonel Pratt's tomb was to be in the lower left. Channel deposit immediately above it.

Pratt's tomb. Pratt was a prominent Catskill tanner and two-term congressman. He had a large number of sculptures carved into the cliff there, all in commemoration of his eventful life. The final carving was the burial vault itself. It cuts right into the base of a Devonian stream channel (figure 8-8). But, for some reason, the vault was never completed; the half-cut vault can still be seen. Nobody knows why the project was abandoned, but one version is that the vault leaked. That may be; the ceiling is composed of a porous-looking litter of fossil Devonian plant debris. Alas, poor Pratt is buried in a cemetery with the common folk, and it may all be because of the odd meandering of a Devonian stream!

The Floodplain Deposits

Bangladesh occupies most of the Ganges Delta and this intensely overcrowded nation suffers from its topography. Unusually rainy monsoon seasons create flood conditions which only get worse as flood waters sweep farther downstream. A flood is a great brown swell, like a huge single wave of water. It rises slowly and ominously, giving people plenty of time to escape. . . or, when there is no escape, plenty of time to contemplate the impending danger. Bangladesh floods are among the worst in the world. Because there is very little elevation anywhere in the country, there are few places to which people might flee. And, because there are enormous numbers of people, the death toll can be horrible.

As flood waters rise, the river channels begin to churn and boil. Unseen river currents tear and erode at the channel sediments, carrying them off as the flood's emblem, brown water. Soon the turbid waters overtop riverbanks and spread out sideways across the floodplain. Floods are destructive but brief; soon the great swell subsides. Waters drain back into the still fast-moving channel flows as the flood crest passes. Flood waters finally slow down, and, as they do, their burden of heavy sediment settles out. Sheets of mud are deposited. Once again the stream bed takes on its usual gluttony of mud and sand. After all of this is over, the pitiless stream resumes its languid meandering to the sea, often

Figure 8-9. River floodplain deposits. Thick ledges are the flood sand-stones, thinner-bedded strata are the floodplain soil horizons.

Figure 8-10: Mud cracked horizon. Mud cracks have been enhanced with water color.

leaving behind a devastated floodplain, with broken forests and a plaster of fresh mud. But the river is heedless and mindless of the deaths it has caused and the damage it has done. Such are the floods that humans record in water-cursed places like Bangladesh.

So too were the ancient floods of the Catskill Delta. Our mountains are haunted by the ghosts of these terrible events, some of them worse than any recalled by humans. All of them are unrecorded except in the rocks, and few of them are remembered except by the occasional geologist. Let's learn how to recognize these, the shades of ancient deluges.

Figure 8-9 shows an outcrop of an ancient Catskill floodplain. The massive, light-colored beds are thick sandstones. These are the flood deposits. At this location they sometimes display fossil tree trunks and branches. It was flooding that must have ripped up some forests in their time. The thinner bedded strata are also the floodplain deposits. Many of these deposits are red colored and those are the soils that developed upon the floodplain during the time intervals between floods. The red color is mostly the mineral hematite.

You can look for a number of other features in a floodplain deposit. One of them is the desiccation crack or, as it is commonly called, the **mud crack**. See figure 8-10. These form when soft, wet mud bakes in the floodplain sun. The sediment dries out and shrinks. Cracks appear and widen as the sediment bakes. The cracks form into polygons, usually of five or six sides. Sometimes the baking process is interrupted by a brief rainfall. When this happens, the few drops that fall can leave tiny craters on the soil surface. Renewed baking hardens the soils and preserves the **raindrop prints** (figure 8-11). I will talk about the fossils of the floodplain in the next chapter, but I should at least mention here the very common **root casts** which are so often seen throughout the red soil deposits of the Catskills (figure 9-8). These fossil tree roots are common in, and characteristic of, the floodplain.

Figure 8-11: Raindrop prints.

Sedimentary Cycles

Most Catskill strata were formed by these river delta streams as they slowly meandered back and forth across their floodplains. But, remember that these floodplains are constantly subsiding and constantly accumulating sediment. It's easy for a river to meander "back," but by the time it meanders "forth" the floodplain has accumulated a lot of new sediment and soil. The new river deposits, trough cross beds and all, end up being deposited on top of the old deposits. Thus, river deposits tend to be stacked into what appear to be depositional cycles. See figure 8-12 which shows the steep topography near Prattsville. Notice the ledges of rocks that appear at various elevations on the slopes of the hill. Each of the ledge horizons is a layer of trough cross bedded river sandstone. The resistant sandstones form the ledges.

It's important for you to understand this because it is fundamental to the understanding of the layered nature of the rocks throughout the heart of the Catskills. As you hike through the mountains, especially as you ascend steep slopes, you will pass through ledges of trough cross bedded strata. You might even see the erosive horizon at its base. That's the base of the cycle. The upper reaches of the cycle are likely to be composed of soft shales that are buried. But farther uphill you will, sooner or later, pass through the sandstone ledge of another cycle. When a complete cycle is exposed, and that is rare, look for the following sequence: The erosional base will be overlain by trough cross beds; then look for a mixture of sheet laminated and planar cross bedded strata. Finally, at the top, you may find ripple marked beds and red floodplain soil horizons. A single sedimentary cycle is called by geologists a **storey** (British spelling).

Figure 8-12: Sedimentary cycles in hillside near Prattsville.
See the horizontal river channel deposits at different levels.

Sedimentary cycles are the single most commonly observed sedimentary feature of the Catskills, so do watch for them. They explain the pattern of ridges and dips along the Glasco Turnpike with which we began this chapter. But more than that, the whole of the Catskills is composed of these cycles. Their sandstone ledges are characteristic of the region. They can be seen on every mountain slope and they give the landscape the appearance of building stories. The Catskills are indeed a storied land.

The Whitewater Streams

The history of the Catskill delta deposits is largely one of meandering streams flowing across a flat delta plain. Behind this plain were the rising Acadian Mountains. Mountain slopes do not have meandering streams or flat floodplains; they have steep slopes with active, whitewater streams. These are erosive, youthful streams with lots of boulders, cobbles and gravel in them. Gravel is especially common. Normally, none of these coarse-grained materials make it onto the delta plain because they are too heavy to be carried that far or they are ground to dust during the journey. Nevertheless, from time to time, conditions do allow their transport onto the delta. Pebbles are commonly found in the upper reaches of the southern Catskill Mountains. If you climb Slide or Panther Mountains, for example, you are likely to see quite a few pebbles mixed in with the sandstones.

Figure 8-13: Closeup of puddingstone.

Puddingstones are different but related lithologies. These rocks are largely gravel with a fair amount of sand and mud mixed in (figure 8-13). They need to be explained. The best theory is that the puddingstones represent episodes of rapid uplift within the Acadian Mountains. As the slopes of these rising mountains steepened, their streams became more able to transport heavy grains of sediment, most of which was gravel. Torrents of white-water cascaded down the slopes and the momentum of these currents carried them out onto the delta plain; with them came the puddingstone gravels.

The Catskill Bluestones

One of the most important economic materials that come out of the Catskills is its famed **bluestones**. The name is a misnomer, for few bluestones are actually blue; most of them range from red to green to brown to gray. All of them are thinly laminated sandstones which break easily into flagstone. Bluestone has long been quarried in the Catskills. The rock is quite resistant to wear and holds up well for long periods of heavy use. Much of it was cut into sidewalk slabs that line our streets today. Bluestone sidewalks are common throughout New York State and many of them are quite old. Bluestone is sometimes cut into building stone as well. Bluestone quarries, old and new, are found throughout the Catskills.

These thinly laminated sandstones form in a variety of environments, most of which were found in the coastal realm of the Catskill Delta. These environments include beaches, offshore sand bars and some environments of deposition within the meandering stream channels. The sheet laminated sandstones of the Catskill river channels are good examples (figure 8-4).

The Blues On a Rainy Night

You have, no doubt, commonly walked the sidewalks on a rainy night. It can be a great pleasure for the young and in love; for the rest of us, it's just cold and wet. But, in the Catskills, a dark, rainy night can bring a journey into the past. You see, many Catskill villages still have old bluestone sidewalks, and each old slab can be a time machine, because it often retains vestiges of its venerable geological past.

Go out, find some bluestone walks and really take a look at them. Many are featureless, but others display sedimentary structures that take us back to moments in the Devonian time. Look for two of these structures. The first is the more obvious; these are the ripple marks (figure 8-14). Devonian-age currents passed across these Devonian sands and sculpted them into delicate ripples. Often the ripples are steeper on one side. That steep side is inclined toward the way the current was flowing. It is a most remarkable experience to visualize these briefest and most ephemeral events of so long ago. They should not exist. And yet, there they are. Were these currents of any special importance? Not at all; they were just the most everyday of events. How could such delicate structures survive long enough to turn into stone?

Figure 8-14: Ripple marked bluestone sidewalk slab.

The other structure is the **flow lineation** (figure 8-15). Again, as currents sweep across sea floors or stream bottoms, they sculpt the sand. This time the resulting feature is virtually invisible. The grains are lined up into a subtle lineation which only appears millions of years later when the stone cutter splits the rock. The resulting fracture has a faint lineation to it.

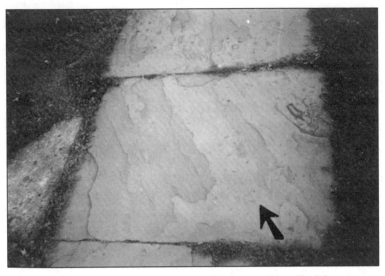

**Figure 8-15: Flow lineations on bluestone sidewalk slab.
Arrow indicates current lineation.**

Both of these features are quite clear in broad daylight and not much harder to see at night, under street lights. But on a rainy night, when the street lights are reflected off the wet sidewalks, these features light up. They are almost electric. It's something to look for anywhere there are bluestones, which includes all of eastern North America.

So you don't have to be young and in love to enjoy a walk on a rainy night. Ripple marks and flow lineations are nice too, although they do come in a distant second place.

The Higher Catskills

Not as much geological work has been done in the higher elevations as down below, probably because it's hard to get up there. Because of this, the highest strata seem to be less well known. These rocks do seem to be different than those below. There is much more gravel throughout the highest reaches of the Catskills, especially the southern Catskills. These gravelly sandstones are also rarely red in color, something commonplace in lower elevations. It has been guessed that these strata represent inland deposits that formed far from the shores of the Appalachian Basin and at elevations above those of the delta plain. These deposits appear to have formed on the slopes leading up to the old Acadian Mountains. We call such deposits **alluvial fans**, and they commonly form today along the bases of mountainous slopes.

Field Trips to the Catskill Delta

North Lake: There is a fine field trip for you to see all of the various types of delta deposits, including the puddingstones. Visit North Lake State Park and take the blue-marked trail north from the lake toward Sunset Rock. On your way to Sunset Rock you will, on two occasions, pass vertically through Catskill sedimentary cycles. These are the stretches where the blue trail goes straight uphill and passes through sandstone ledges. As you climb through a cycle, watch for the red shales, which were floodplain soils. You may see some fossil root casts in them. The red soils are abruptly cut into by the trough cross beds of the river sandstones.

Sunset Rock is perched upon a high promontory of rock with a knockout view of the Hudson River Valley. But before you reach it, the blue trail takes you below and behind this mass of rock, and this is where you will see walls of puddingstone. The rock is most impressive; it is a mixture of coarse gravel and cobbles. Look the pebbles over carefully and you will see that quartz pebbles are among the most common. But there are a large number of different types of pebbles to be seen. All of these are the different types of rocks that made up the ancient source lands of the Acadian Mountains. In the North Lake vicinity, there are a number of other locations where river deposits and puddingstones can be seen.

Throughout the rest of the Catskills the hiking trails will take you through many sandstone ledges. Watch for all of the typical river deposit structures: Trough cross beds, sheet laminations, planar cross beds, and sometimes ripple marks. Most trails will eventually take you into the highest elevations of the mountains. Watch, as you climb uphill, and you will see that the red color disappears while the pebbles of puddingstone conglomerate become more common.

Overlook Mountain: Many abandoned bluestone quarries can be seen along the old Overlook Mountain Road and it is well worth the hike. Overlook Mountain Road was once an important road, but it is now part of the Catskill Forest Preserve and is thus only a hiking trail. Go to Plattekill Clove and pick up the red trail off Prediger Road. Take the red trail southeast and turn onto the blue trail, which is the old Overlook Mountain Road. It hugs the crest of the mountain. There are many old and overgrown bluestone quarries along the trail. Another good way to explore the stratigraphy of Overlook Mountain is to approach it from the south. From the Glasco Turnpike, turn up Meads Mountain Road and park at the trailhead. A hike up to the top of Overlook Mountain can illustrate much of what this chapter has been about. This is a popular hike and you may have made it before, but you didn't know the stratigraphy then, so let's see if a little bit of knowledge doesn't change your perspective.

Just a short distance up the trail, at the registration box, you will find the first ledge of thick-bedded river sandstone. The resistant sandstone stands out alongside the trail. Notice the trail itself, which has a gray tint to it. Now, as you continue upwards, watch for a change in the color of the trail. The gray is followed by a brick red; the trail has crossed from the river sands to the red shales. The shales are not to be seen; they are so soft that they are rarely exposed. Farther up, the trail becomes gray again and more sandstones can be seen on either side. This is, of course, followed by another red stretch of the trail.

This sets the pace for the rest of the ascent. The color of the trail alternates between red and gray. The gray stretches are usually lined with outcrops of river sandstone. The red stretches mark the unseen fossil soils, too soft to make outcroppings. It's like climbing through a building; each gray/red couplet takes you through a single "story" and, as you climb Overlook, it is only natural to start counting them. The stories provide a history, if you know how to read it. The third story was a massive sand-stone; you can envision the great river that was once here. There are large numbers of pebbles in the sandstones of the 14th story. They tumbled down the steep slopes of the Acadian Mountains at a time when those mountains had started to rise actively. At the 23rd story, you can find large cobbles in the river sands. The old Acadians had by then risen to very high elevations and now even cobbles were tumbling down their steep slopes. What a wondrous thing it is to be able to read a history of a long-lost mountain range in the sandstones of a mountain trail! In the 27th story you finally get a good look at the elusive fossil red soils. There are fossil casts of tree roots there, and we get a glimpse of the old Gilboa Forest that once lived at the base of the Acadian Mountains. The 30th and final story is below the fire tower at the top of the mountain.

And so knowing a little about how to read the stratigraphy of Overlook Mountain can certainly give you some new insights about the old mountain. The stories that the stories tell are of the old Catskill Delta. The delta lay just about at sea level and was continuously subsiding. Thirty times rivers meandered back and forth across the Overlook site, and 30 times they plastered down layers of sand. And 30 times red soils formed behind the passing rivers. It took a long time for these events to happen, and Overlook Mountain records it all.

Chapter Nine

The Land of Gilboa

ON SUNDAY, October 3, 1869, a great storm crossed the coast near Washington, D.C. It's not clear whether it was a hurricane or a northeaster, but over the next two days it whipped up the coast, passing through eastern Pennsylvania, Connecticut, eastern Massachusetts, Maine and finally Nova Scotia. The storm was enormous and left a trail of devastation. The Catskills were out of its direct path, but they received a lot of heavy rain. Many bridges were washed away, including an important one across Schoharie Creek at the village of Gilboa. It would cost the town $10,000, but the bridge was needed; it was quickly rebuilt and ready for use by January of 1870.

In excavating for the bridge abutments, workmen discovered several large fossil tree stumps in the bedrock. They were still standing upright, in place, as they had been for nearly 400 million years. This was our first view of an important early fossil forest. The stone arboretum must have excited the human imagination and conjured up all sorts of mental images. That's a normal human reaction. This was the discovery of an ancient landscape that I will refer to as the **"land of Gilboa."**

The land of Gilboa is the landscape of the Catskill Delta. We have seen that the Appalachian Basin formed by subsidence of the crust that accompanied the uplift of the Acadian Mountains. Those mountains weathered and eroded and produced the sediments of the Catskill delta complex. Sand and mud began to fill in the basin, turning a marine habitat into a terrestrial one. Like the Ganges Delta of Bangladesh, this was a low-lying landscape, just barely above sea level. It was wet and much of it would have been swamp and bayou. Both fast and sluggish streams must have criss-crossed this delta. There were many ponds, large and small. It was tropical, and the land of Gilboa was certainly a very fine habitat for the plants and animals of the time.

Plants of the Gilboa Forest

The most famous paleontology of New York State is probably that of the Gilboa Forest. When it was discovered, after the flood of 1869, this was the oldest known fossil forest, and its discovery was the cause of great excitement. Since that time many more tree stumps have turned up in the Gilboa vicinity. The biggest discovery occurred in 1920 along the Schoharie Creek just below today's reservoir dam. There, in a location called the Riverside Quarry, about 200 tree stumps were excavated.

It's quite a scene to imagine (figure 9-1). These ancient forests were made up of tall, exotic-looking trees. They were not the trees we are so familiar with today: There were no flowering deciduous trees or cone-bearing evergreen trees. These Devonian

Figure 9-1: The Gilboa Forest. This reconstruction was in the old State Museum.
Courtesy New York State Museum.

forests were of very primitive forms. They represent grades of evolution extending from the most primitive of the land plants to levels just above that of the fern. For the most part, these early land plants were so simple that they did not have proper leaves or root systems, but they were at least composed of wood and had tall trunks.

The discoveries of 1869 were of a species that came to be called by its Latin name, *Eospermatopteris*. The trees were preserved as stumps and partial trunks that had been buried, quite likely during a Devonian flood. The upper reaches of the trunks and all of the branches were lost, but fortunately an extensive fossil foliage was found associated with the stumps. These branches probably belong to the trunks, but, as that cannot be proved, they go by a different Latin name, *Aneurophyton*. Most people lump the stumps and foliage together and call the whole assemblage by the name *Eospermatopteris* (figure 9-2).

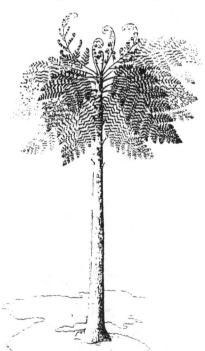

Eospermatopteris belonged to a group of plants called the **progymnosperms**. Essentially, that means that these plants had traits which indicated that they were related to both ferns and gymnosperms (conifers and ginkgoes). Specifically, their foliage resembled that of ferns and produced spores as ferns do, while their trunks were woody and resembled those of conifers. Try to imagine a large fern with the trunk of a pine tree.

Another form of progymnosperm that is commonly found in the Catskills is *Archaeopteris*

Figure 9-2: The Gilboa tree,
Eospermatopteris.
Courtesy New York State Museum.

(figure 9-3). This is an important form, for it is thought to be the ancestor of today's conifers. Our Christmas trees had their counterparts in the land of Gilboa!

Many of the other trees of the land of Gilboa belonged to a group called the **lycopsids**. There are more than a half-dozen species of lycopsids known from the Catskill Delta. A good example is *Lepidosigillaria*, better known as the "Naples tree," named for the location where it was found (figure 9-4). Lycopsids are characterized by very nice diamond-shaped leaf scars on their lower trunks (figure 9-5). The upper lycopsid trunk and all the branches had small, scale-like, primitive leaves. On this basis, they are sometimes called "**scale trees.**"

The really primitive fossil land plants of the Catskills are the **psilophytes** (figure 9-6). These were among the first of the world's **vascular plants**, plants that had vascular tissue (xylem and phloem) that allowed them to draw

Figure 9-3: Archeopteris.
Courtesy New York State Museum.

Figure 9-4: The Naples tree,
Lepidosigillaria.
Courtesy New York State Museum.

111

Figure 9-5: Leaf scars of a lycopsid.
Courtesy New York State Museum.

Figure 9-6: A psilophyte.

water out of the ground and thus survive on the land. The land of Gilboa must have had its share of lichens and mosses as well. But I don't believe that many, if any, of these are found as fossils.

The fossils of the Gilboa Forest are common enough. As you follow the hiking trails into the Catskills you will climb over ledges of sandstones. Occasionally, the broken litter of sandstone blocks will yield bits of tree trunk. Most of the time these fragments are of small-diameter trees, but, on rare occasions, you will find a fine, thick trunk. Preservation is the biggest problem. Fossil wood of this sort just does not preserve well. Too often, it was partly decayed by the time it was buried. Nevertheless, you will have little difficulty in recognizing it.

Figure 9-7: Fossil stumps of Gilboa trees at Gilboa.

There is a fine display of Gilboa tree stumps in Gilboa itself (figure 9-7). It's just downstream from the Schoharie Reservoir dam, very close to the old Riverside Quarry. Take Rt. 30 and travel 2.8 miles north from Grand Gorge. Turn right and go downhill another 1.2 miles and you will reach Schoharie Creek. There, in a small park, is a display of half a dozen fossil stumps of *Eospermatopteris*. The rest of the 200 that were found here are scattered throughout colleges and museums all over the country.

Fossil wood is rare, but there was no problem with the preservation of the tree roots. Even after they decayed they often came to be well preserved. Soils fill in the root casts and they harden into fine fossils (figure 9-8). These fossils, sometimes called **rhizomorphs**, are found throughout the Catskill red sediments.

Animals of the Gilboa Forest

The Gilboa Forest grew within the Catskill Delta, flourishing along the banks of the delta's rivers. The concept of a forest ecology was a new one during the Devonian. Land plants had only recently evolved and there were even fewer land animals. There weren't many suitable habitats for animals at this early time in the colonization of the land. One of the habitats that did exist was within the soils beneath the forests. Here there was a lot of partially decayed plant matter, called detritus, which served

Figure 9-8: Root casts from the Gilboa Forest.

as food for an assemblage of small, primitive land animals. We call them **detritivores,** and they, in turn, served as food for an assemblage of small **carnivores.**

Among the detritivores were the **earthworms.** These soft, delicate creatures left few, if any, fossils, and we don't know exactly what they looked like, but they were probably much like today's worms. Most of the remaining detritivores were primitive arthropods. We have already seen some of the marine arthropods (Chapter Seven), but there were also quite a few on the land. The soils of the land of Gilboa would have been rich in **centipedes** and **millipedes,** feeding upon the organic detritus.

Most Devonian arthropods were very small. They include the earliest of the six-legged arthropods, the **insects.** Devonian insects had not yet evolved flight and instead crawled around sluggishly within the soils. Today's **bristletails** resemble these ancient forms (figure 9-9). The modern silverfish is among the bristletails. You have probably seen these many times. When you get a chance, stop and take a good close look at one of the humble creatures. They belong more to the Devonian than to the present.

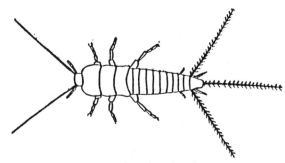

Figure 9-9: Modern bristletail.

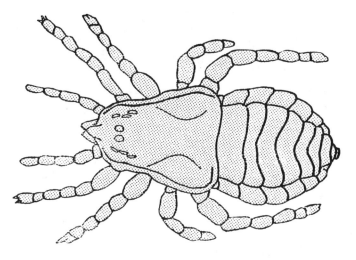

Figure 9-10: A trigonotarbid.

The detritivores were simple creatures that lived simple lives. I am not sure that they were capable of such things as fear. But if they could manifest fear, there would have been good reasons to do so. There was, for example, the mighty **trigonotarbid** (figure 9-10). This great beast was the saber-tooth tiger of the land of Gilboa. One can imagine this mighty predator in action. Its complex eyes must have scanned the landscape for a meal. Its slim, spider-like legs would have propelled it rapidly toward its intended victim. Its sharp jaws would have quickly sliced up and dispatched its hapless prey. Triumphant, the mighty trigonotarbid would have swaggered off in search of its next meal. Of course I should mention that the fearsome trigonotarbid was the size of a pea! Other predators included the **spiders** and a group called the **pseudoscorpions**. All in all, Gilboa did have its share of Lilliputian carnivores.

The land of Gilboa must have had a deafening silence. There were no birds, no roaring animals, and even the insects were mute. On a windless day it is hard to imagine that any noise echoed out of the Gilboa forests. Hike into the high Catskills on a quiet day in November, after the songbirds are gone and the insects have died. That's when you can experience a forest silence which only begins to approach that of the Gilboa. November's forest is gray and dead, so silence seems sensible, but the Gilboa Forest was alive and vivid with green, and the quiet would have seemed all wrong there. But the noise-makers had yet to appear.

Aquatic Life

Much of the animal life of the Gilboa Forest was found within the ponds and rivers of the Catskill Delta. Their fossils are not common, but they are interesting. The rarest and certainly the most prized fossil finds among the Gilboa arthropods are the **sea scorpions** or **eurypterids**. Despite their name, several types of sea scorpions inhabited the fresh-water rivers and ponds of the Catskill Delta. See figure 9-11 for a painting of them by the famous painter of fossils, Charles Knight. The largest was nearly five feet long (figure 9-12); none of them was very small.

One interesting form that I mentioned earlier is *Isopodichnus* (figure 7-18), that enigmatic set of footprints from an early arthropod. Sometimes found in near-shore, dark Hamilton shales, it's small, but it can also be found with diligent searching in the fine-grained, floodplain deposits of the Catskill Delta.

Among my favorite delta animal fossils is a trace fossil that records moments of danger, terror and suspense. This is the "escape" burrow of the clam *Archanodon catskillensis* (figures 9-13 & 9-14). You will remember from Chapter Eight that the Catskill Delta was prone to flooding. As flood waters rose, the rivers became erosive. Later, as each flood subsided, the river bottoms became depositional. None of this presented any problem for a

Figure 9-11 (above): Eurypterids, from
a painting by Charles Knight.
Courtesy New York State Museum.

Figure 9-12 (right): The eurypterid.
Courtesy New York State Museum.

Figure 9-13 (below): The clam *Archanodon*.
Courtesy New York State Museum.

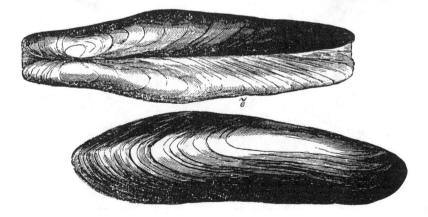

Figure 9-14 (left):
Escape burrow of the
clam *Archanodon.*

Figure 9-15 (below):
Trace fossils left by a
colony of *Archanodon.*

Facing page.

Figure 9-16 (top):
Cephalaspis.

Figure 9-17 (second):
Dipterus.

Figure 9-18 (third):
Holoptychus.

Figure 9-19 (bottom):
Ground pine or club
moss, a lycopod.

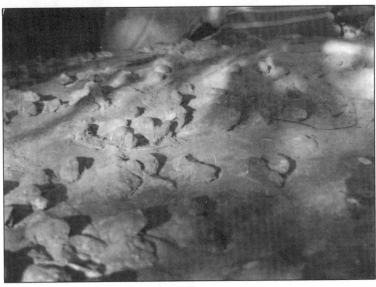

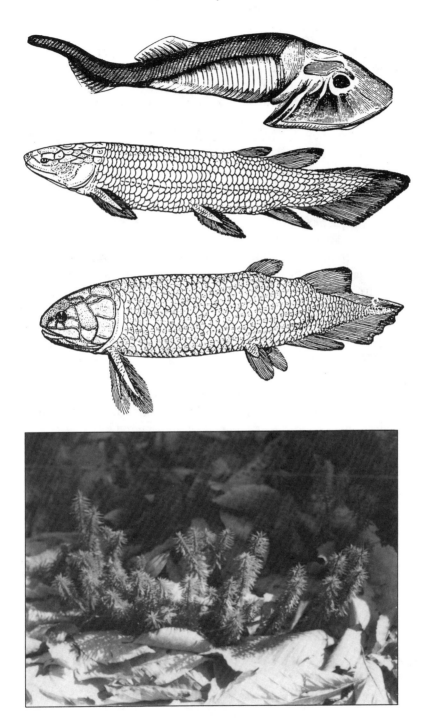

river, but, for its inhabitants, these could be times of real danger. Floods commonly affected the river-dwelling clams. In good times, dense colonies of these clams lived on the floor of delta rivers (figure 9-15). Flood erosion, however, would transport great masses of sand down the river and post-flood deposition would bury whole colonies under several feet of sediment. A three-inch-long-clam under three feet of sediment is in serious trouble unless it can escape by burrowing upward; *Archanodon* could do just that. The escape burrows are common and easily recognized. The desperate clams inched their way through overlying sediment until they reached the new floor of the river and survived. They almost always succeeded.

Plenty of fish lived in the freshwater habitats of the Catskill Delta, and they belonged to several interesting and important groups. Some of the earliest and simplest fish lived here. *Cephalaspis* is a good example (figure 9-16). It's a member of an early fish group called the **jawless fish**. They lacked a lower jaw and had no teeth. They had, at best, only one pair of fins and, all-in-all, were very primitive forms indeed. There were also placoderm fish, with their toothless jaws, in the Catskill Delta.

Fish were rapidly evolving at that time, and there were modern fish types as well. These are called the **bony fish**. They had both jaws and teeth. They had a pretty good bite and hence their evolutionary success. Some of the most progressive of these were called the **lungfish**. A good example is *Dipterus* (figure 9-17). These were remarkable fish in that they probably had fully functional lungs and could breathe air. This was an important advantage for a group of fish who lived in waters that were likely to dry out during the common droughts of the late Devonian. During droughts, when the oxygen content of water was reduced, they could breathe air and survive. They had another strategy for when it got worse; they would burrow into the muds and go into a state of suspension called estivation. When the waters returned, they would awaken and go about their lives again.

A second strategy for droughts was employed by a special group of lung-bearing fish, the **crossopterygians**. These creatures were characterized by unusually strong and sturdy paired fins. Many of them could probably drag themselves around on land with these fins. A good Catskill example is *Holoptychus* (figure 9-18). See the large forward fins on this fish. Crossopterygians could, in case of drought, drag themselves off in search of another pond or river. This strategy was an important one, for it was these walking and breathing fish who evolved into the amphibians, who, in turn, eventually evolved into the land-dwelling reptiles and mammals.

Gilboa Today

It is a wonderful thing to imagine the great images that emerge from the old land of Gilboa. But it doesn't have to be entirely a matter of imagination; you can go out and visit the land of Gilboa today. Roam the forests of the Catskills on a nice day in the late summer. It won't take long to find what's left of Gilboa, and that is a great deal. There are the lichens and the mosses. They are common and beautiful elements of the flora, especially on the rock ledges of the Catskills. They are primitive, probably very little changed from their Devonian ancestors. Then there are the **lycopods**, modern lycopsids that are still here. We call the most common forms **ground pine** or **club mosses** (figure 9-19) and you will find them everywhere. Take a good look at them; they have those primitive leaves that were typical of the Devonian forests.

Kick an old, dead log. Most of the time you will disturb some unhappy centipedes and very likely a few millipedes as well. Here too are creatures who are little changed from their ancestors who were here a little less than 400 million years ago.

There are no crossopterygians or lungfish in today's Catskill lakes and rivers, but there are freshwater clams virtually unchanged from the *Archanodon* clams of the Devonian.

All these odd creatures are called **living fossils,** and that's a good name. Living fossils are whole groups of organisms who have evolved so little that they remain virtually unchanged from perhaps hundreds of millions of years ago. They comprise a peep hole through time and give us invaluable insights as to what their ancient ancestors were like.

And these living fossils speak to us of how important those Devonian times were and of the great biological events that were occurring back then. The land of Gilboa was in a time and place where life was rapidly evolving. The trees were advancing quickly and the very concept of forest ecology was developing for the first time in earth history. Also evolving on the floors of those forests were the assemblages of insects, spiders and other arthropods that have been so important ever since that time. And then there were the vertebrates. We have seen how the fish were diversifying and rapidly evolving into the modern forms. The land of Gilboa was about to produce the amphibians, and from them would come all of the other vertebrate forms, and that includes us. Yes, our family tree very likely includes the fish, possibly the very crossopterygians that inhabited the land of Gilboa.

Chapter Ten

An Elevator Through Time

OUR elevator jumps abruptly and begins descending once more. It is carrying us downward toward an even older land. Our ride is a short one and we soon come to another halt and the south-facing door opens. This is not the Devonian time period but the older Silurian. Out there is a very shallow sea, so shallow that we can see the bottom. It's a quartz sea. That is, the sediments are the purest of sands; almost all the grains are of white quartz and the sea floor is gleaming with a crystalline glow.

Now the south door closes and the east door opens. Out there is a broad, white quartz sand beach. Beyond it, in the distance, rises a hilly landscape, the remnants of a once-taller terrain. There were once great mountains here, but they have crumbled. In the end, quartz sand is the fate of all mountains. The door closes and, once again, down we go.

Another short ride soon ends and all four doors open. It is 450 million years ago. We have left the Silurian and have now gone back even further: To the Ordovician time period. We are surrounded on all four sides by the waters of a deep sea. Off to the far east a great mountain range rises on the horizon. These mountains, called the Taconics, are mostly blue and gunmetal-gray. They show no hint of green; there is no foliage on these lifeless peaks. The Ordovician was long over and the Taconics long gone before plants successfully invaded the land.

This is time travel as only a geologist can know. There are endless cycles to nature; nothing is permanent. These Taconics came before the Acadians, and the Grenvilles came before the

Taconics. The days and the seasons come and go. The years pass by and generations are born into, and die from, this world. Nothing stays forever. Climates change; deserts appear and disappear; glaciers expand and melt away. Nothing is permanent; oceans rise and fall and continents drift across the surface of the globe. Nothing remains the same, even mountains. Our elevator ride has taken us on a path first traveled by James Hutton. It has shown us mountains and oceans that once existed and are now gone. We have seen plants and animals that are long gone. Nothing is permanent; five billion years from now Earth itself will be swallowed up by an expanding sun.

But now, before us, an Ordovician breeze quickens and blows across the sea. For a moment there is a chop to the water, but it soon subsides. What is more ephemeral than a breeze? The elevator doors all close.

Index

2

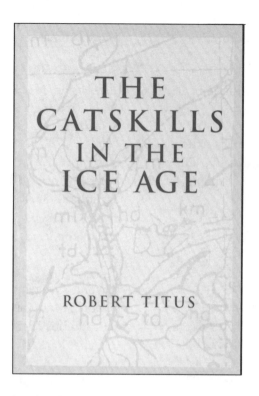

THE
CATSKILLS
IN THE
ICE AGE

ROBERT TITUS

A sequel to *The Catskills: A Geological Guide*

The Catskill Mountains as we know them today are the legacy of the massive forces unleashed in the last ice age. Virtually all mountain communities are built where they are because glaciers made some of the land habitable; our best agricultural lands are the floors of glacial lakes; much of our recreational hiking and climbing leads to scenery carved by the passing ice. The glaciers that covered these mountains did not in themselves produce art, literature, or environmental ethics, but here they created a setting that inspired all three. This is the story of *The Catskills in the Ice Age*. Available at bookstores or from the publisher.

For a free catalog of more than 300 books about New York State history, natural history, folklore, the arts, and outdoor recreation, write Purple Mountain Press, Ltd., P.O. Box E3, Fleiscumanns, NY 12430-0378; or call 914-254-4062, or fax 914-254-4476; or e-mail Purple@catskill.net. Visit our website at http://www.catskill.net/purple.